W9-CCY-642

IF I GO
Missing

To all those who feel invisible — you are valued and you are loved.

— Brianna Jonnie

Published in Canada in 2019. Published in the United States in 2020.

James Lorimer & Company Ltd., Publishers acknowledges funding support from the Ontario Arts Council (OAC), an agency of the Government of Ontario. We acknowledge the support of the Canada Council for the Arts, which last year invested $153 million to bring the arts to Canadians throughout the country. This project has been made possible with the support of Ontario Creates.

Cover design: Tyler Cleroux
Cover illustration: Nshannacappo

Library and Archives Canada Cataloguing in Publication

Title: If I go missing / text by Brianna Jonnie and Nahanni Shingoose ; art by Neal Shannacappo.

Names: Jonnie, Brianna, author. | Shingoose, Nahanni, author. | Shannacappo, Neal, illustrator.

Identifiers: Canadiana 20190130695 | ISBN 9781459414518 (hardcover)

Subjects: CSH: Native women—Crimes against—Canada—Comic books, strips, etc. | CSH: Native women— Violence against—Canada—Comic books, strips, etc. | CSH: Creative nonfiction, Canadian (English) | LCGFT: Graphic novels.

Classification: LCC PN6733.J66 I35 2019 | DDC j741.5/971—dc23

Published by:
James Lorimer & Company Ltd., Publishers
117 Peter Street, Suite 304
Toronto, ON, Canada
M5V 0M3
www.lorimer.ca

Distributed in Canada by:
Formac Lorimer Books
5502 Atlantic Street
Halifax, NS, Canada
B3H 1G4

Distributed in the US by:
Lerner Publisher Services
1251 Washington Ave. N.
Minneapolis, MN, USA
55401
www.lernerbooks.com

Printed and bound in South Korea.

IF I GO Missing

Text by Brianna Jonnie and Nahanni Shingoose
Art by Nshannacappo

James Lorimer & Company Ltd., Publishers
Toronto

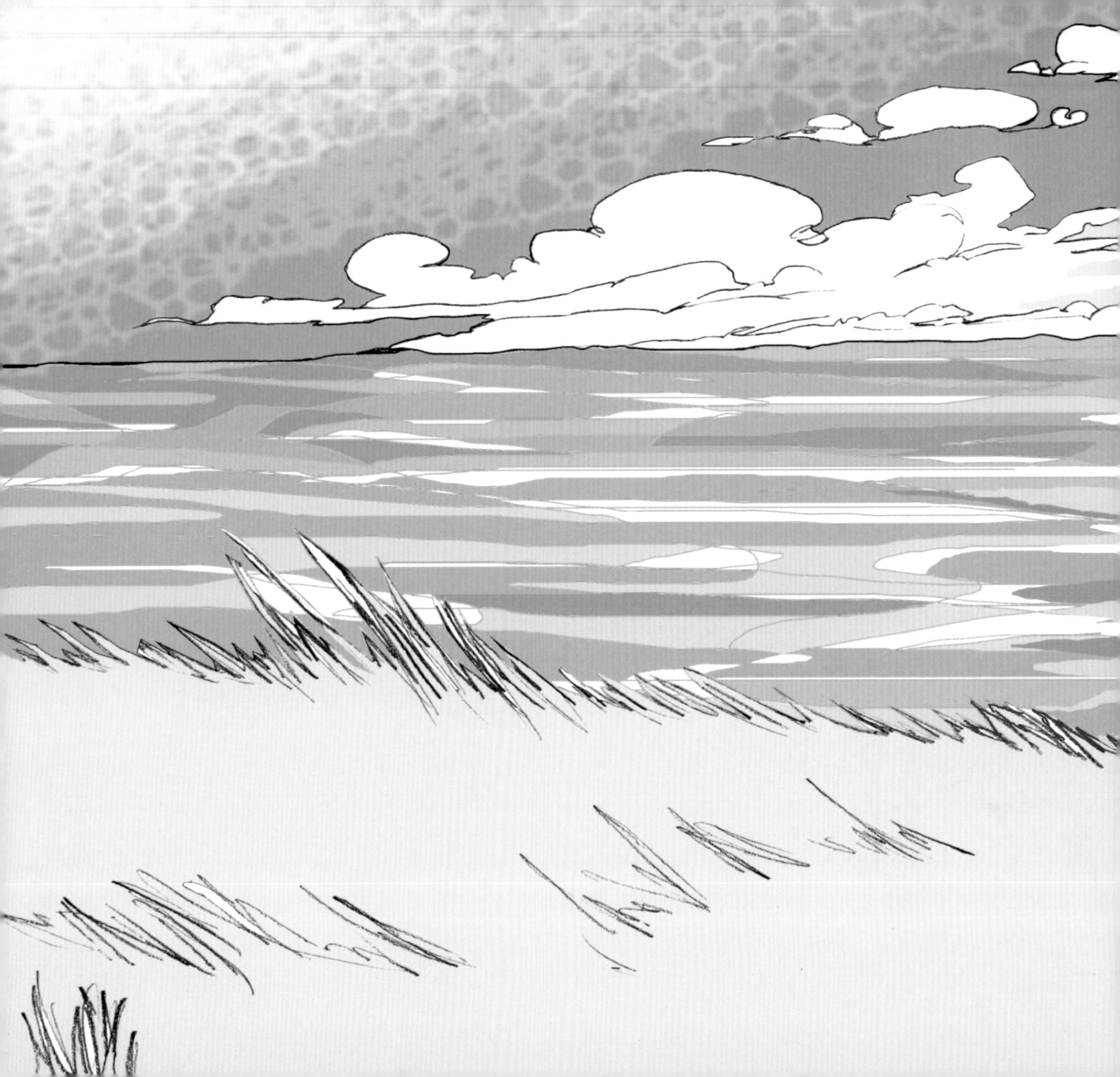

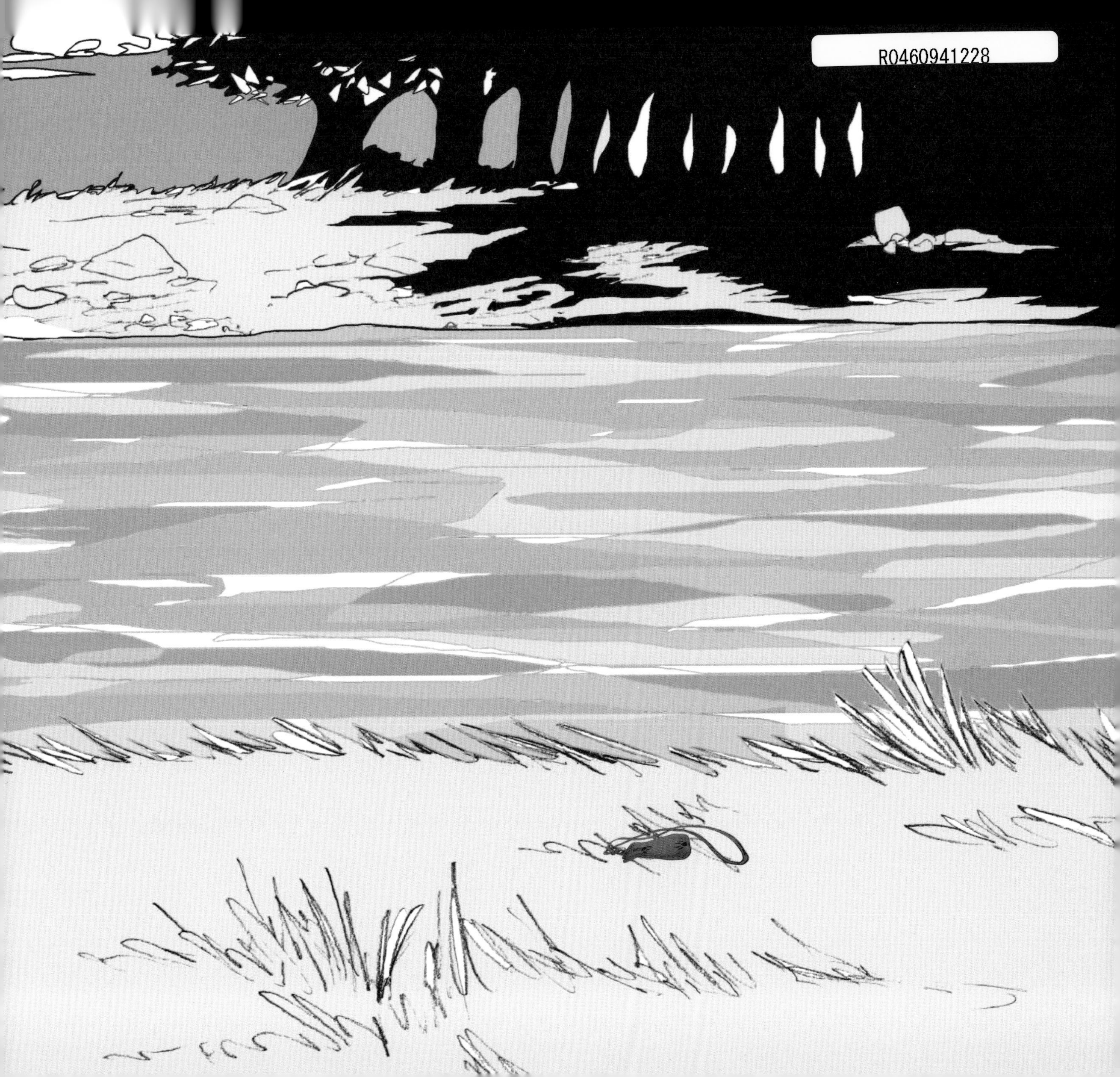

United Nations Declaration on the Rights of Indigenous Peoples states:

Governments, with proper consultation with Indigenous peoples, will ensure Indigenous elders, women, youth, children and persons with disabilities have their rights respected. Governments will ensure that Indigenous women and children are free from all forms of violence and discrimination.

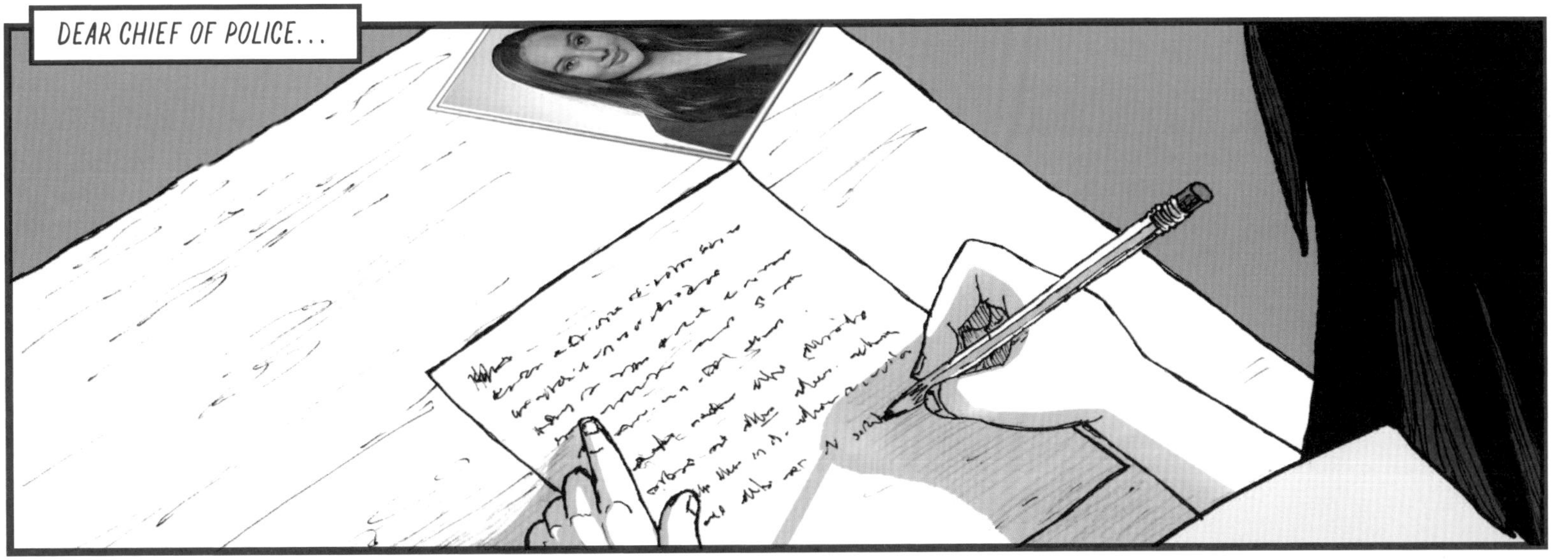
DEAR CHIEF OF POLICE...

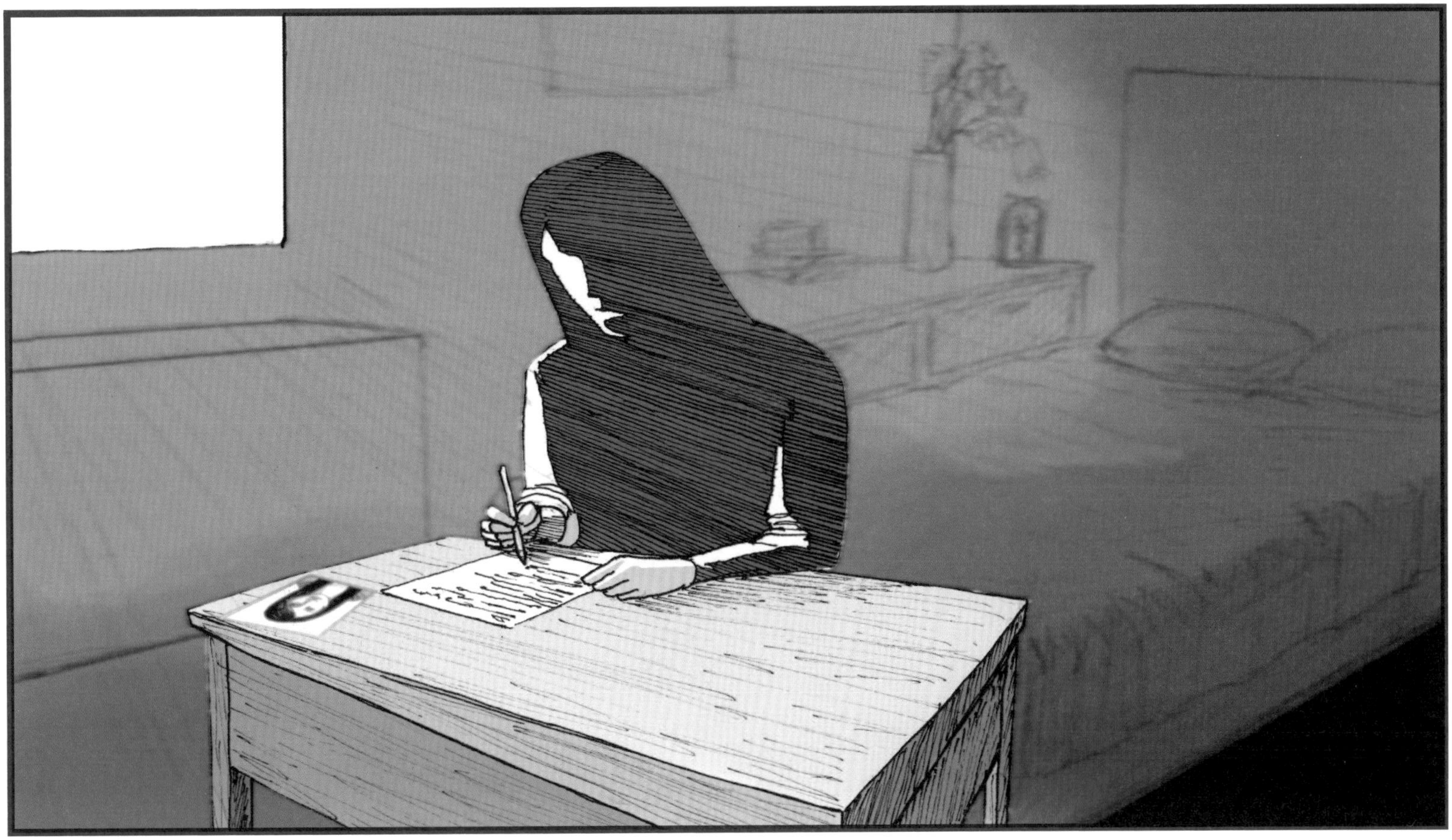

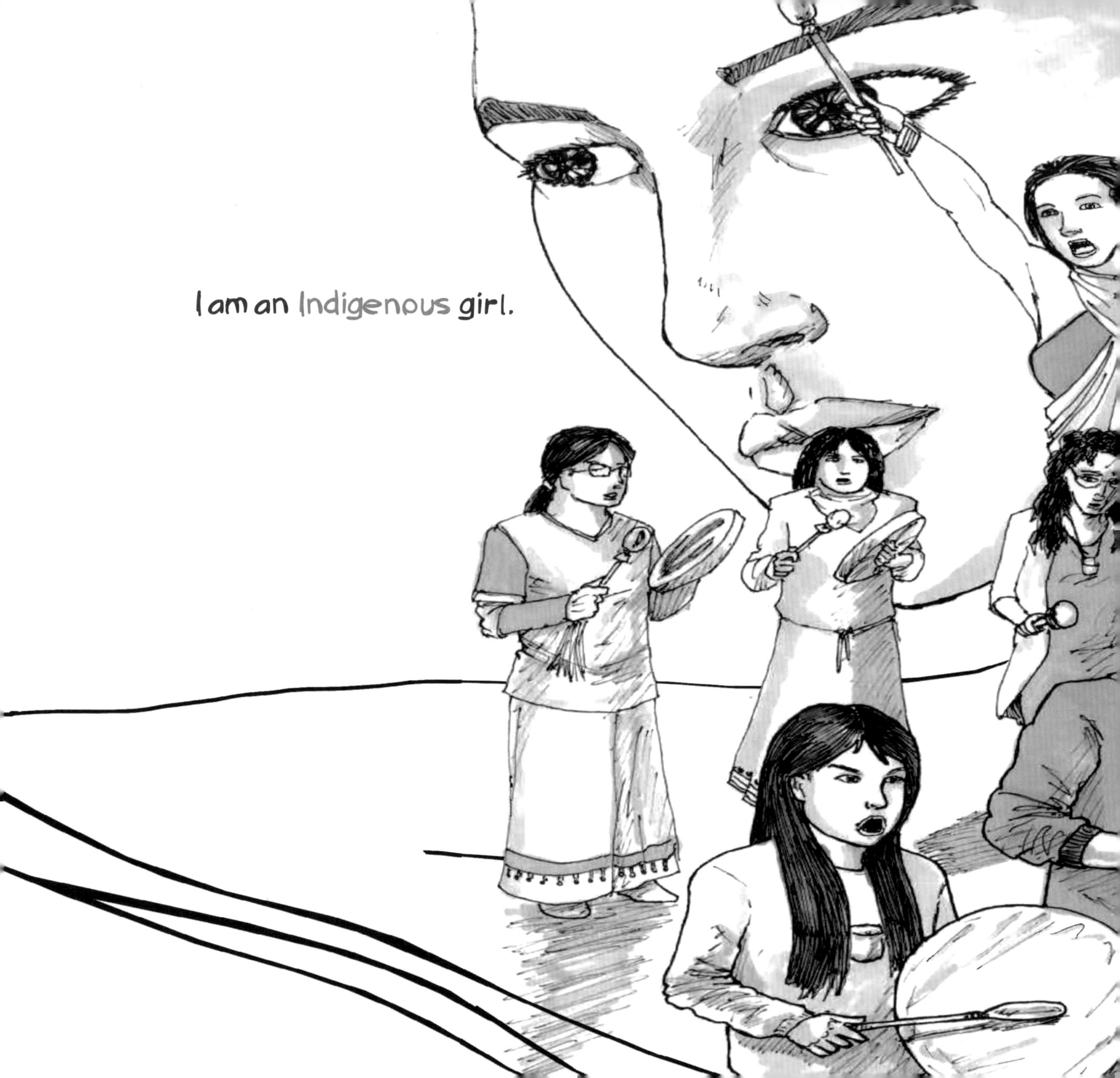

I am an Indigenous girl.

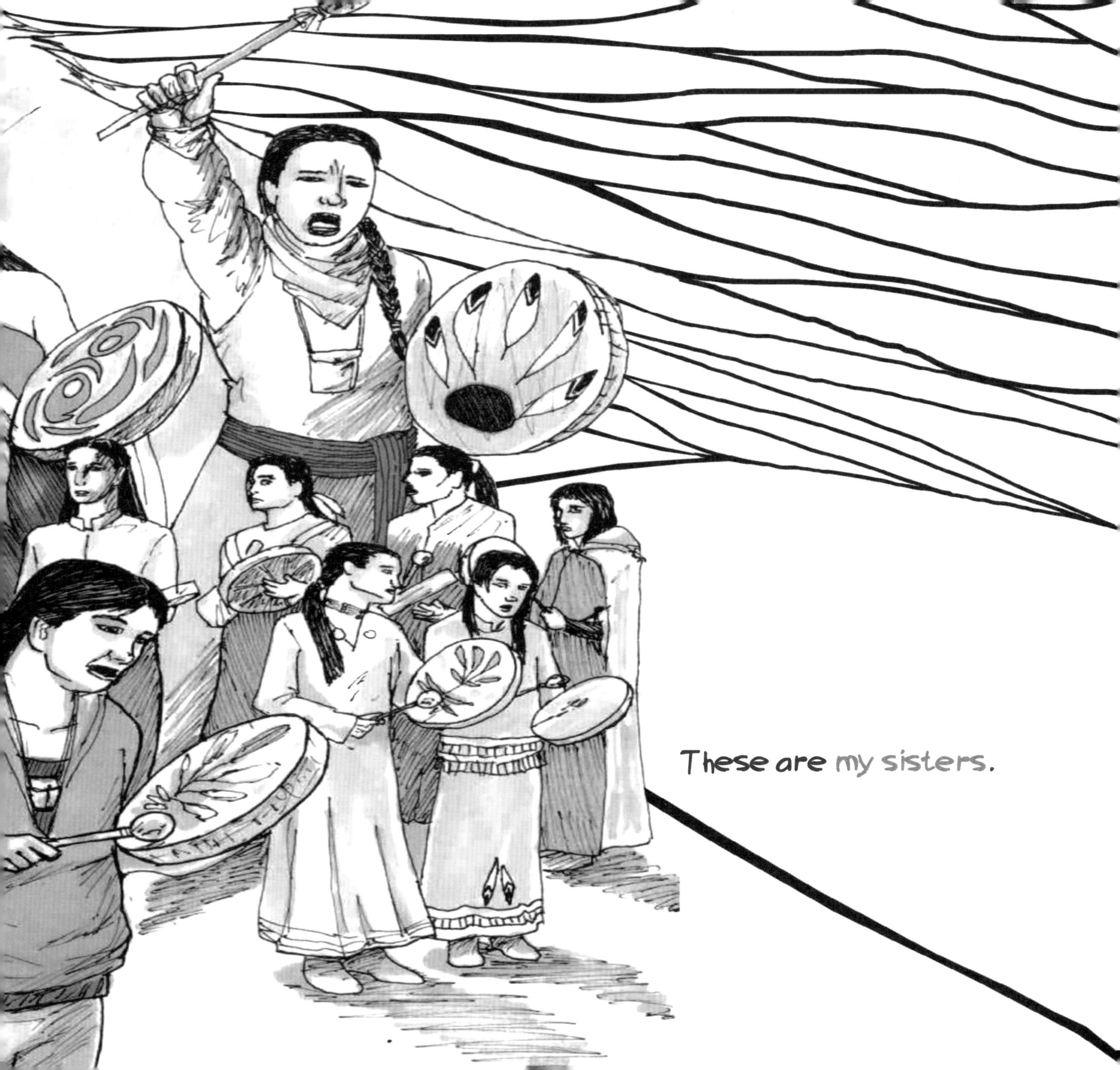

These are my sisters.

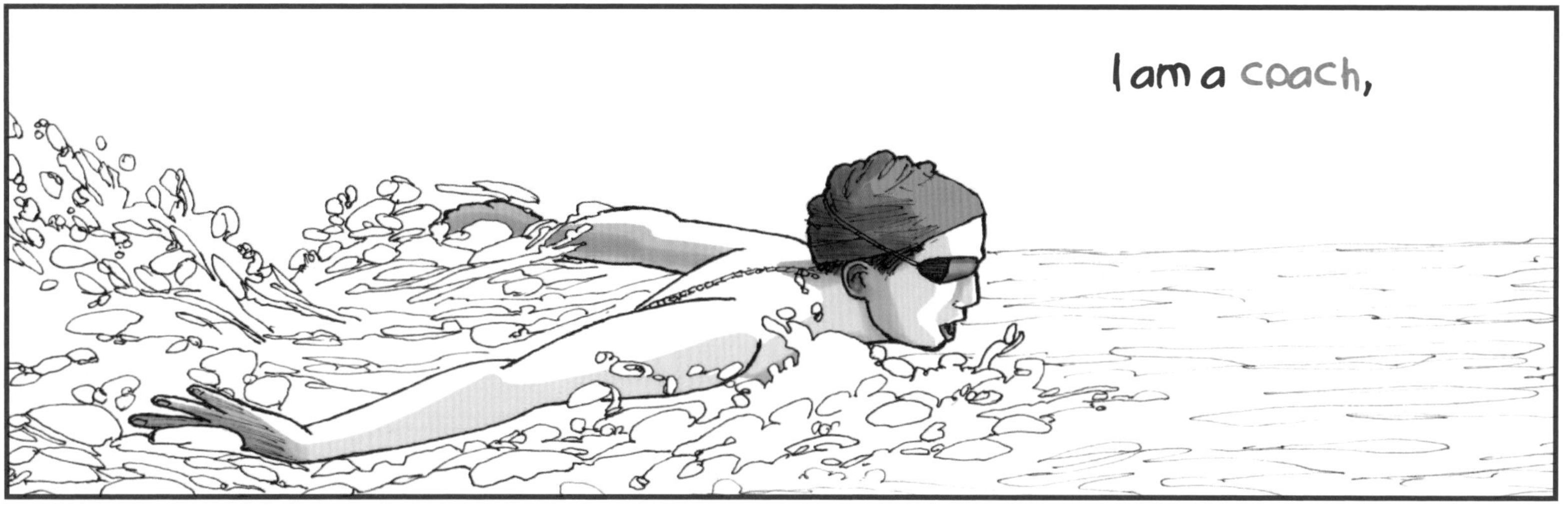
I am a coach,

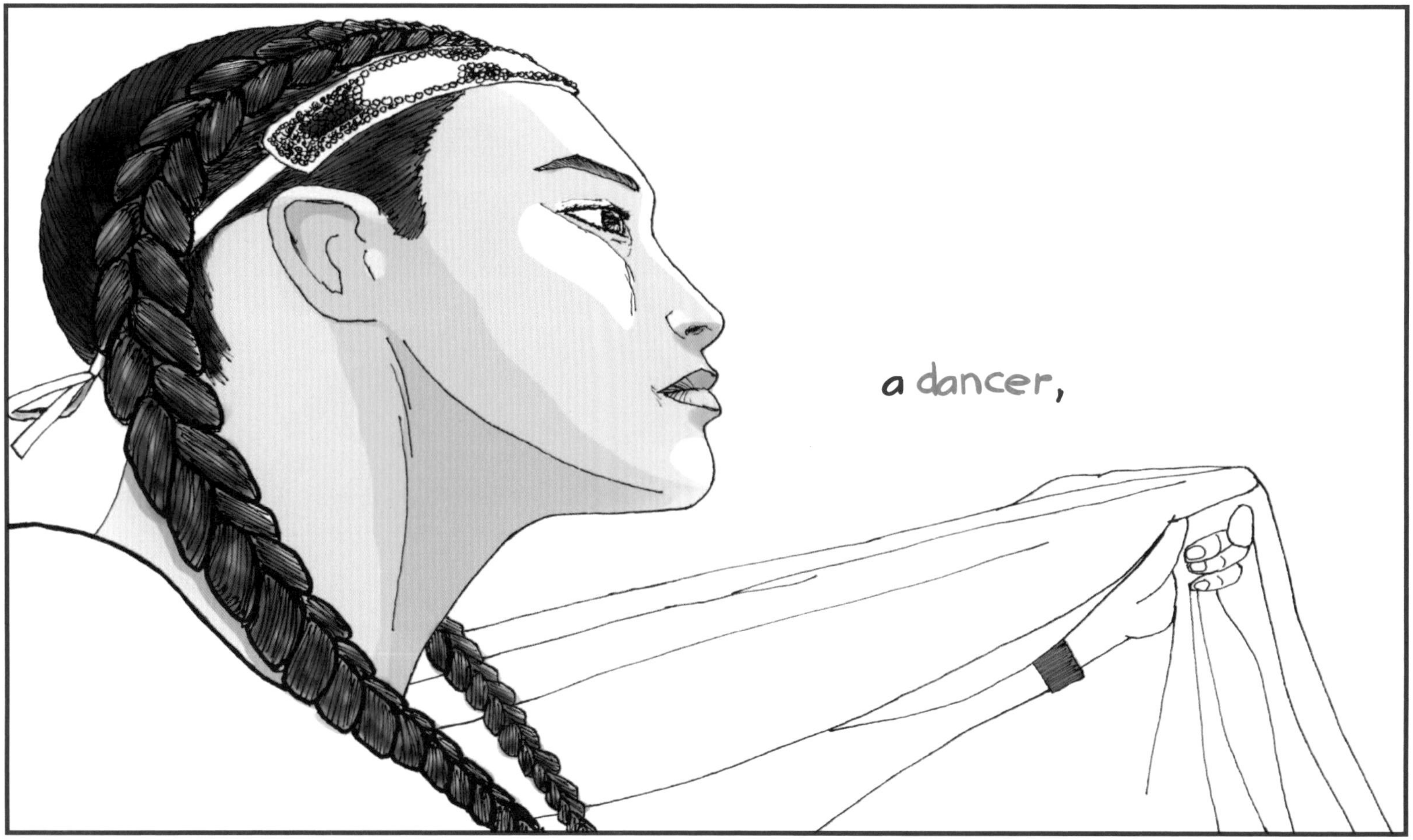
a dancer,

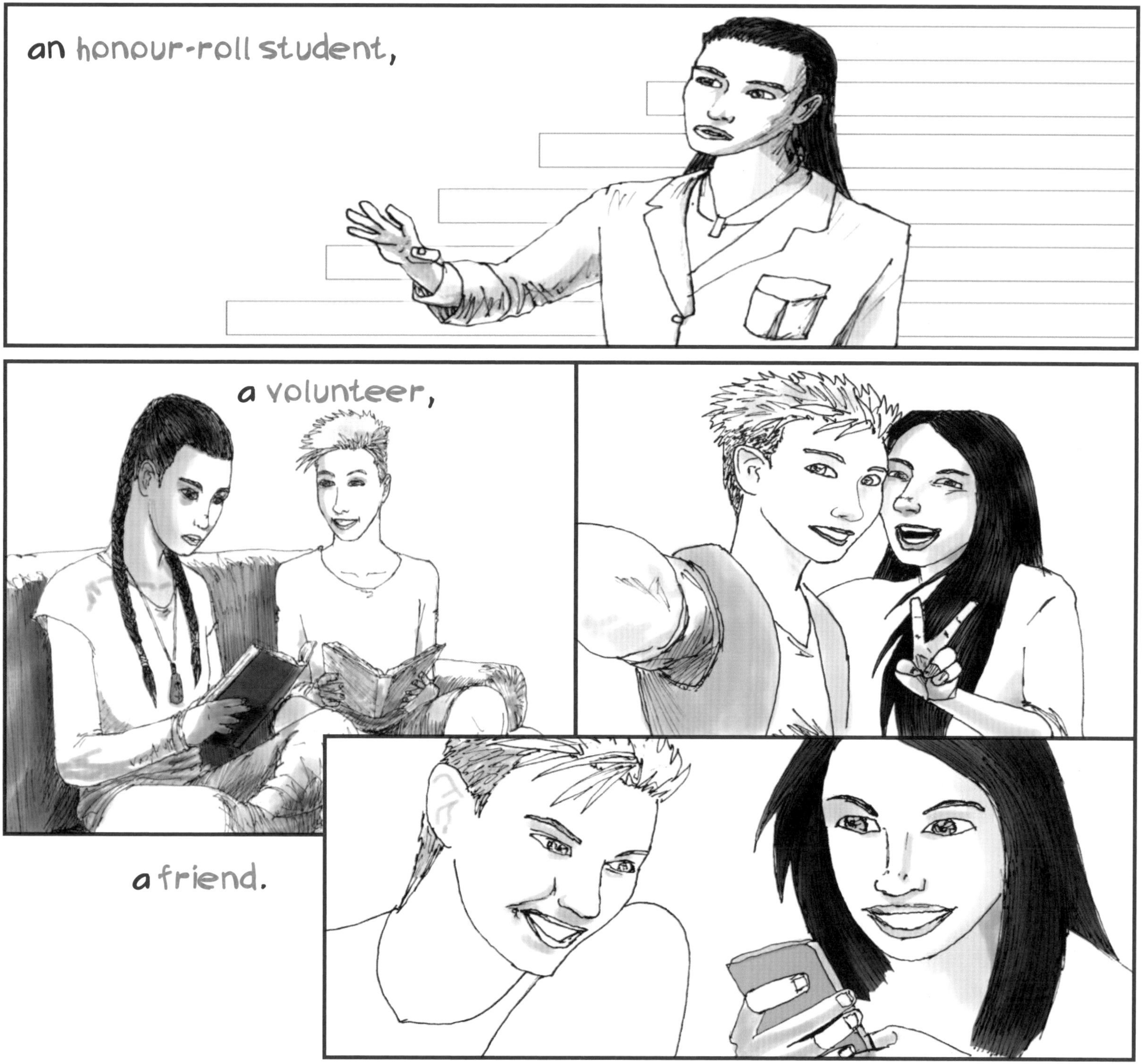
an honour-roll student,
a volunteer,
a friend.

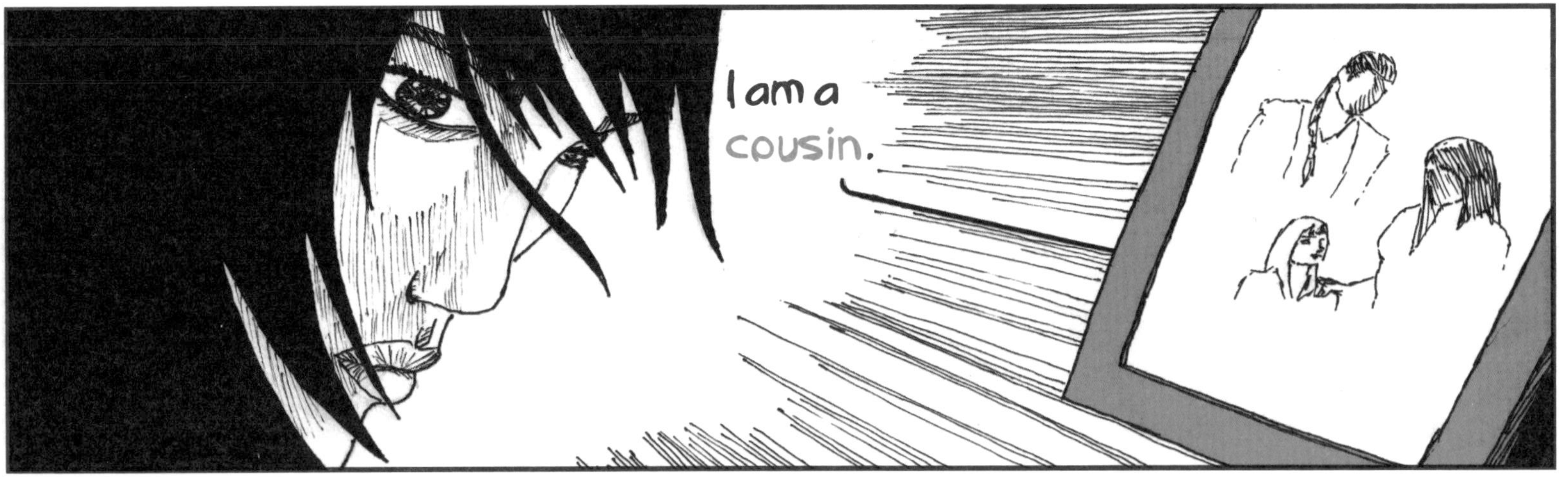
I am a cousin.

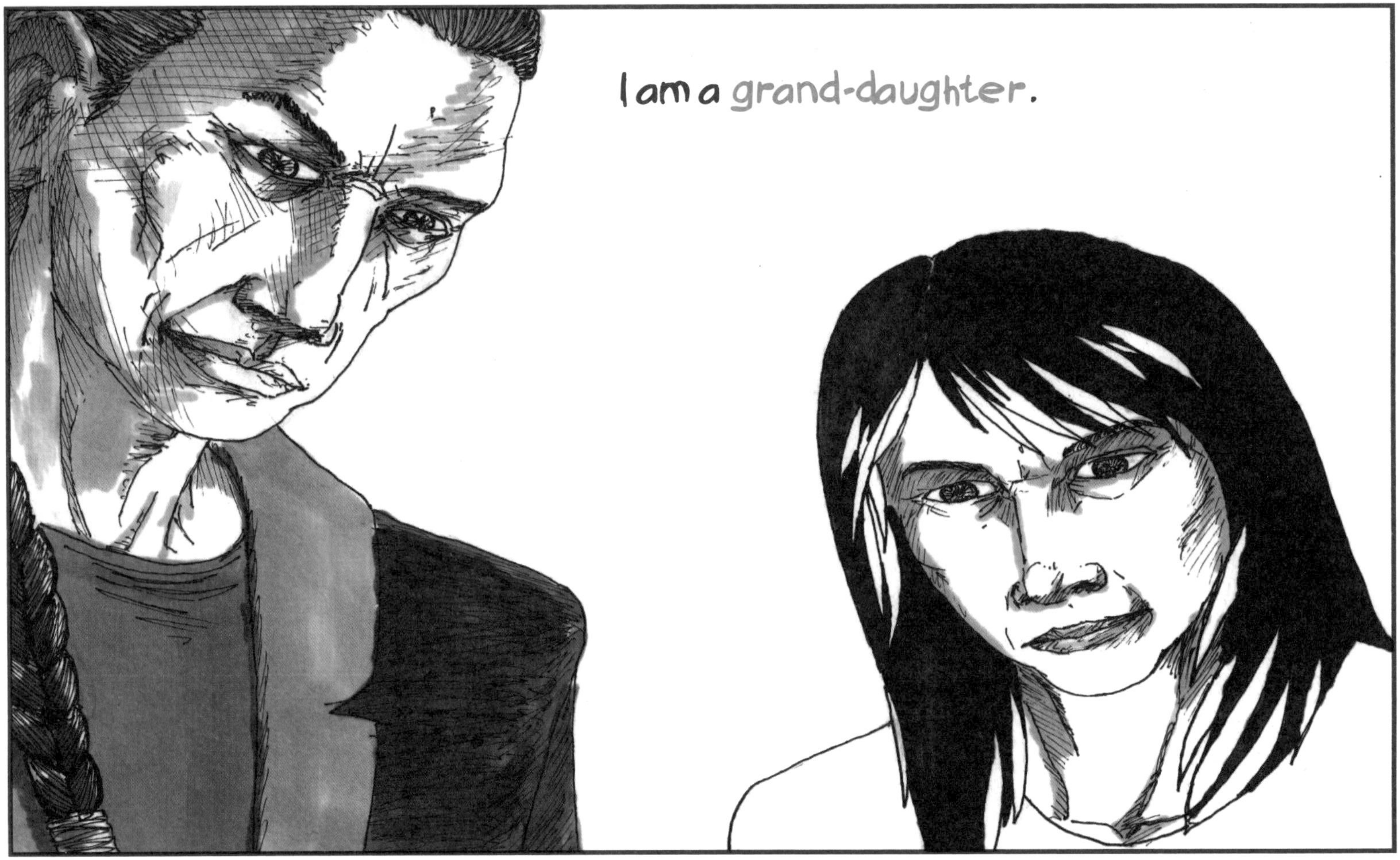
I am a grand-daughter.

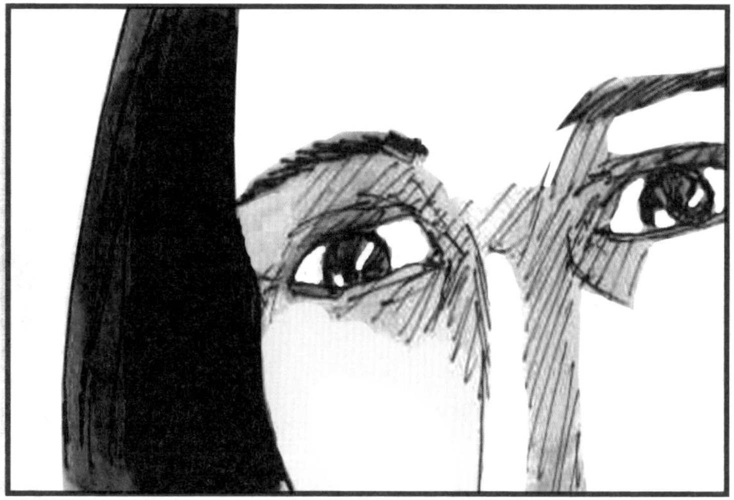

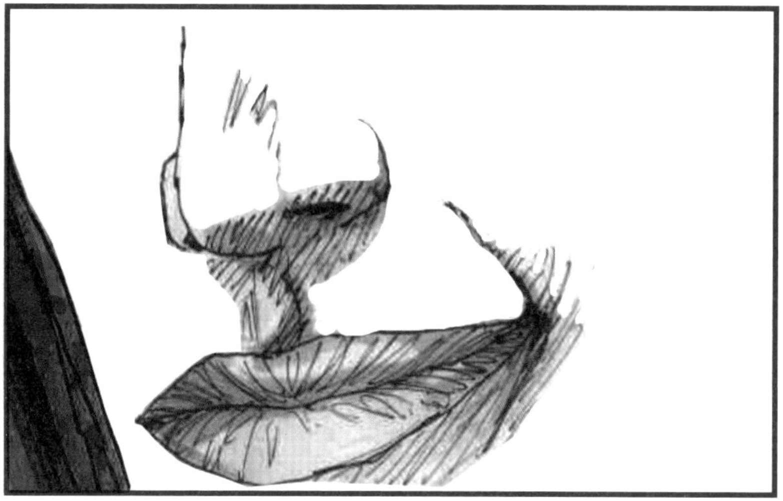

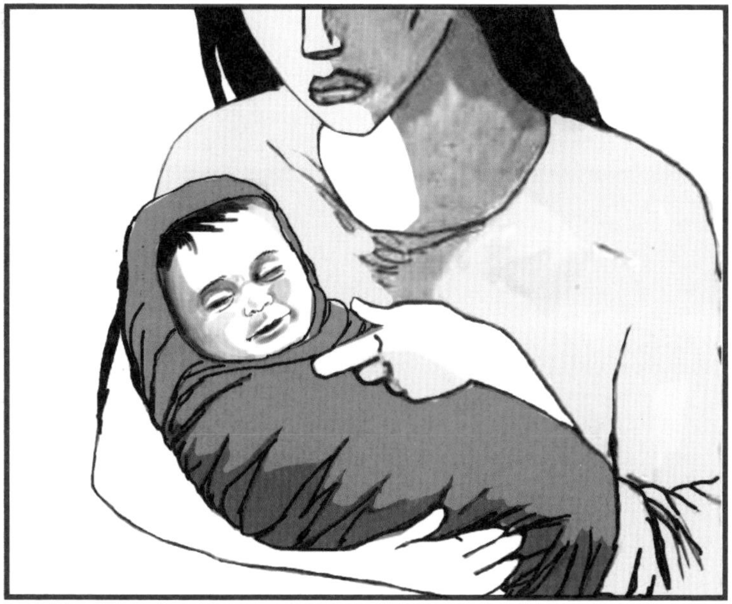

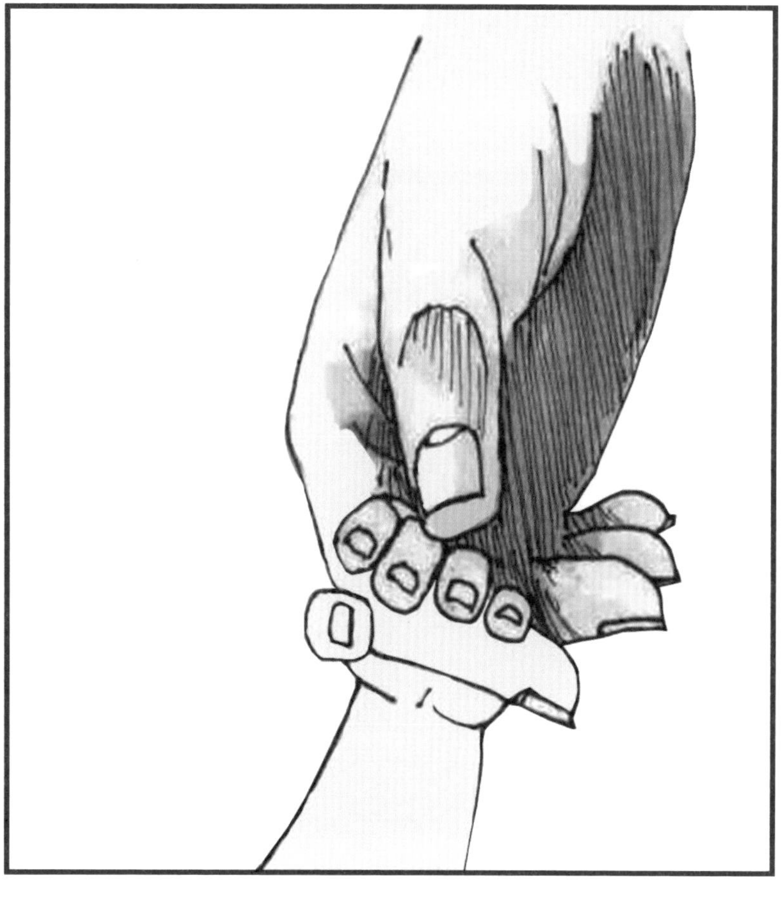

I am a daughter...

... to a young, single mom who loves me more than humanly possible.

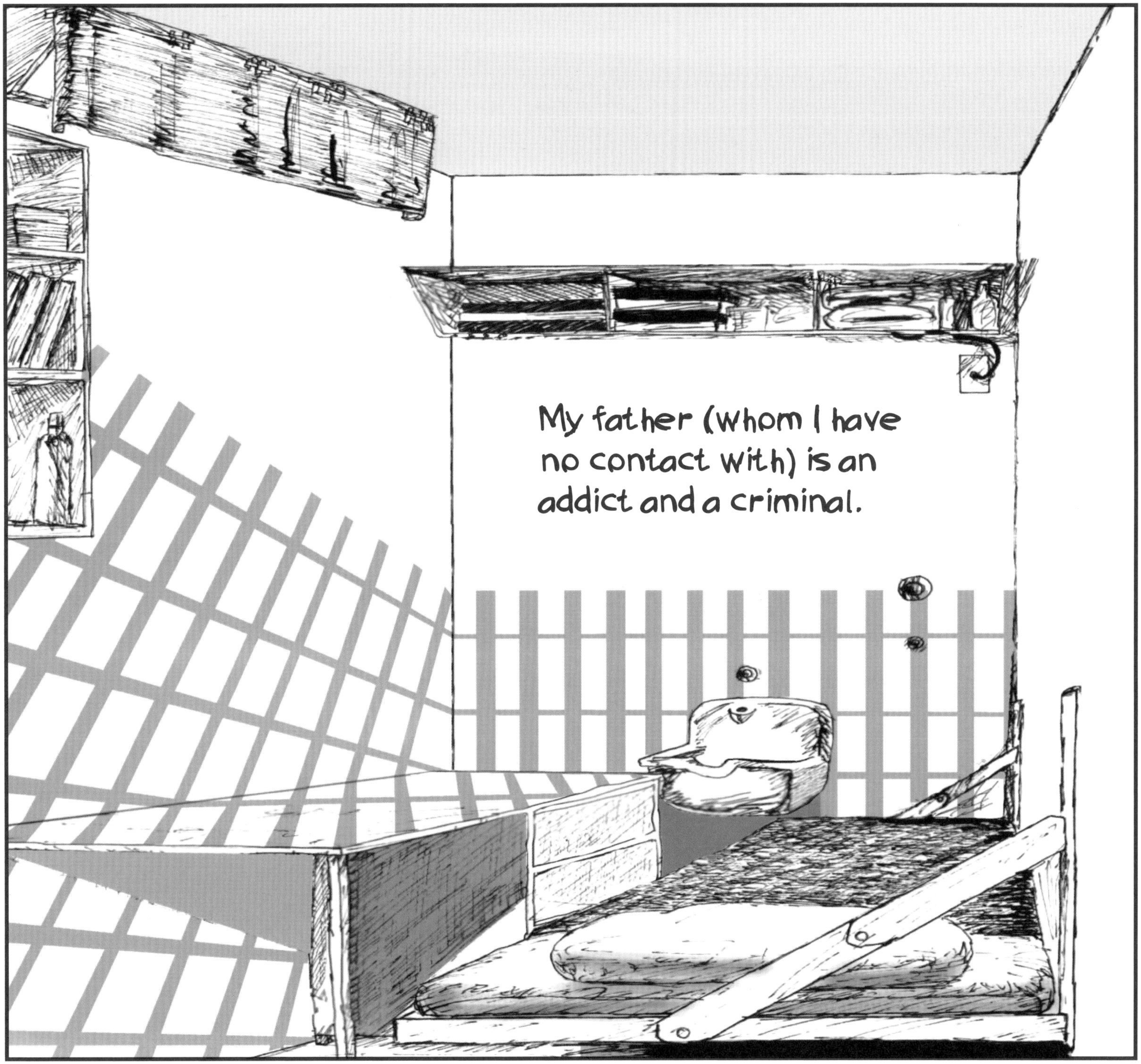
My father (whom I have no contact with) is an addict and a criminal.

I am not involved in drugs,

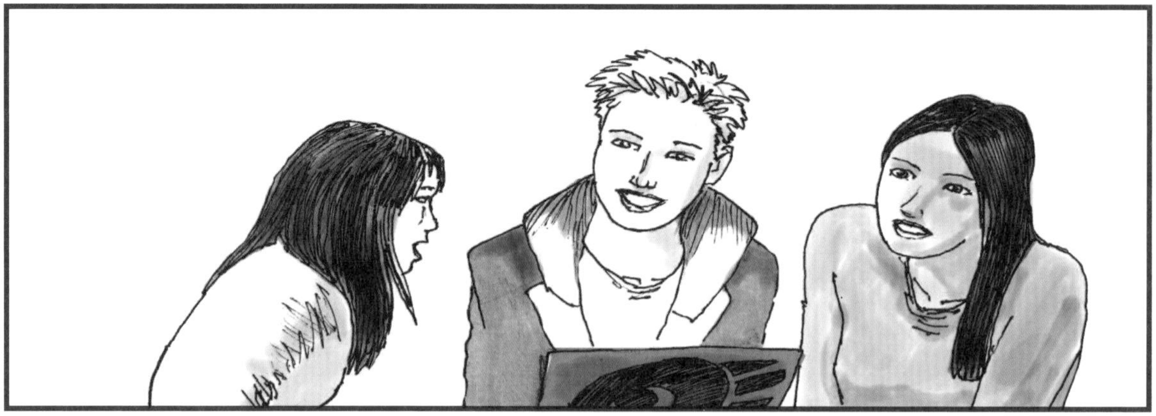

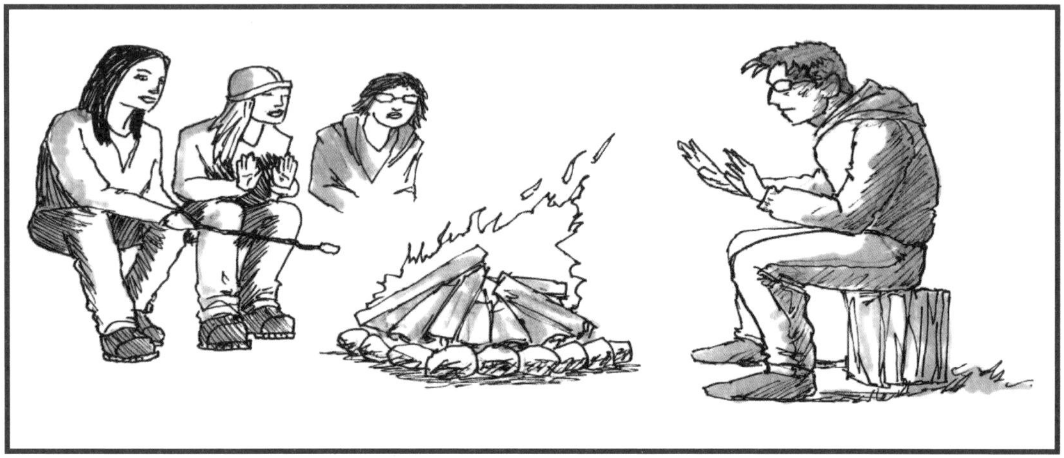

underage drinking, prostitution

or other illegal activity.

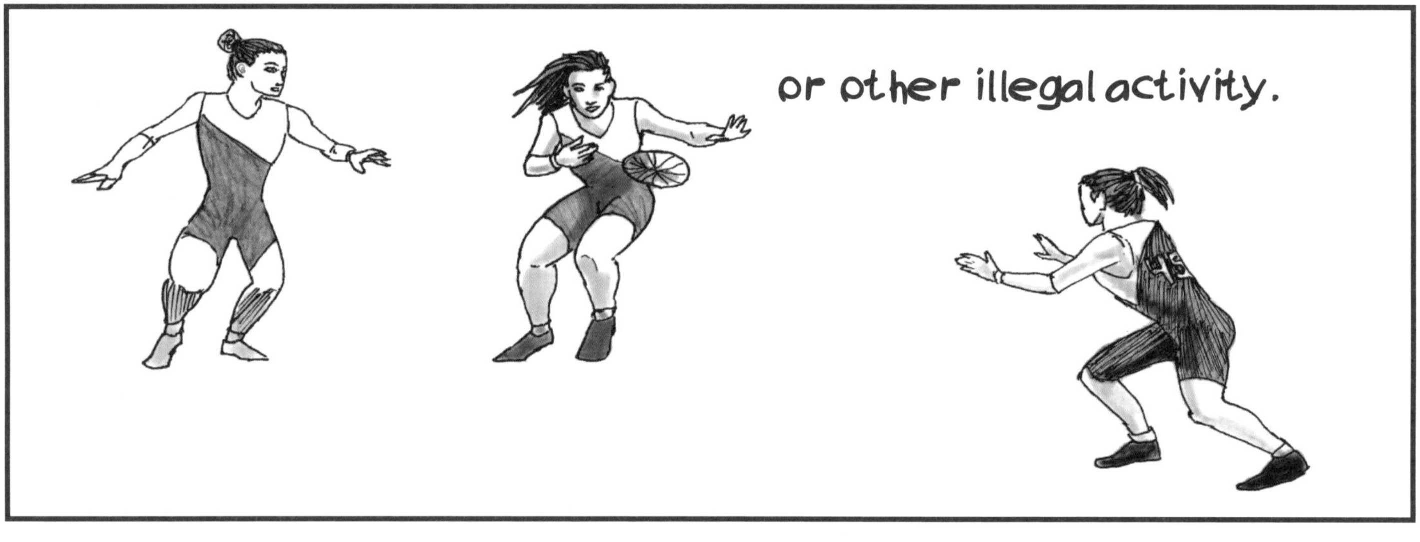

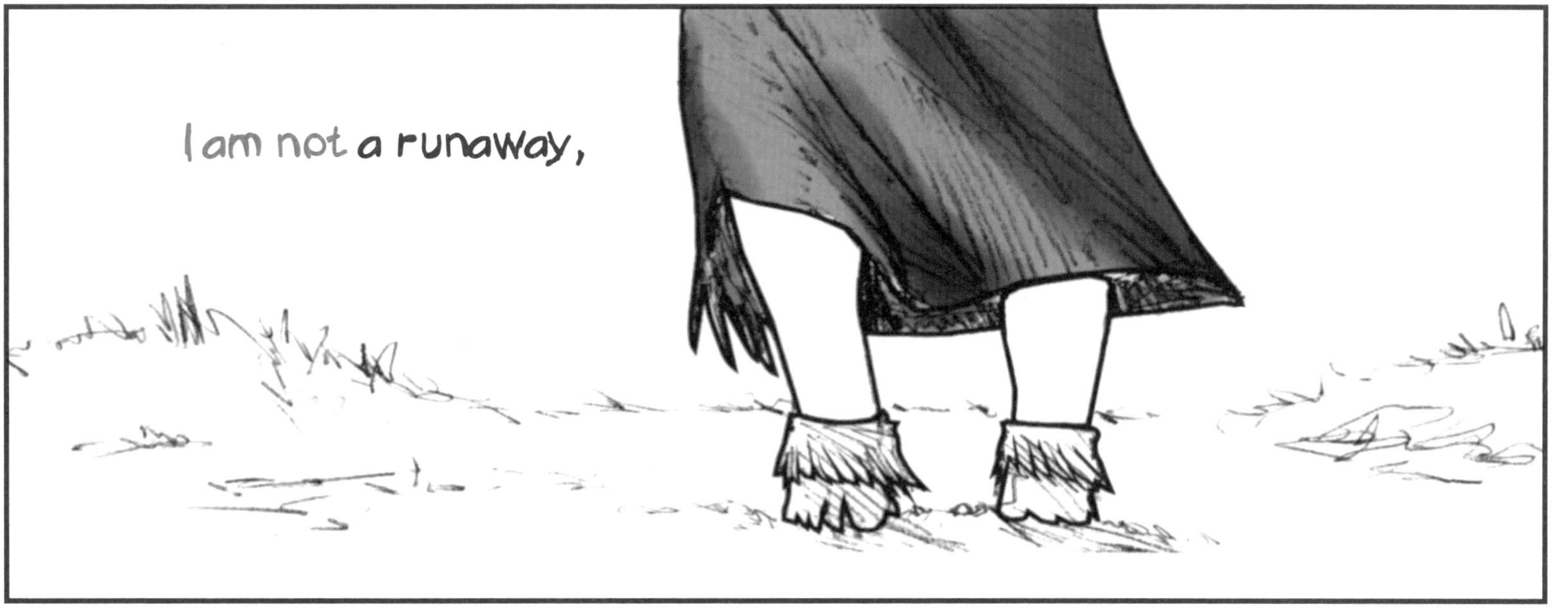
I am not a runaway,

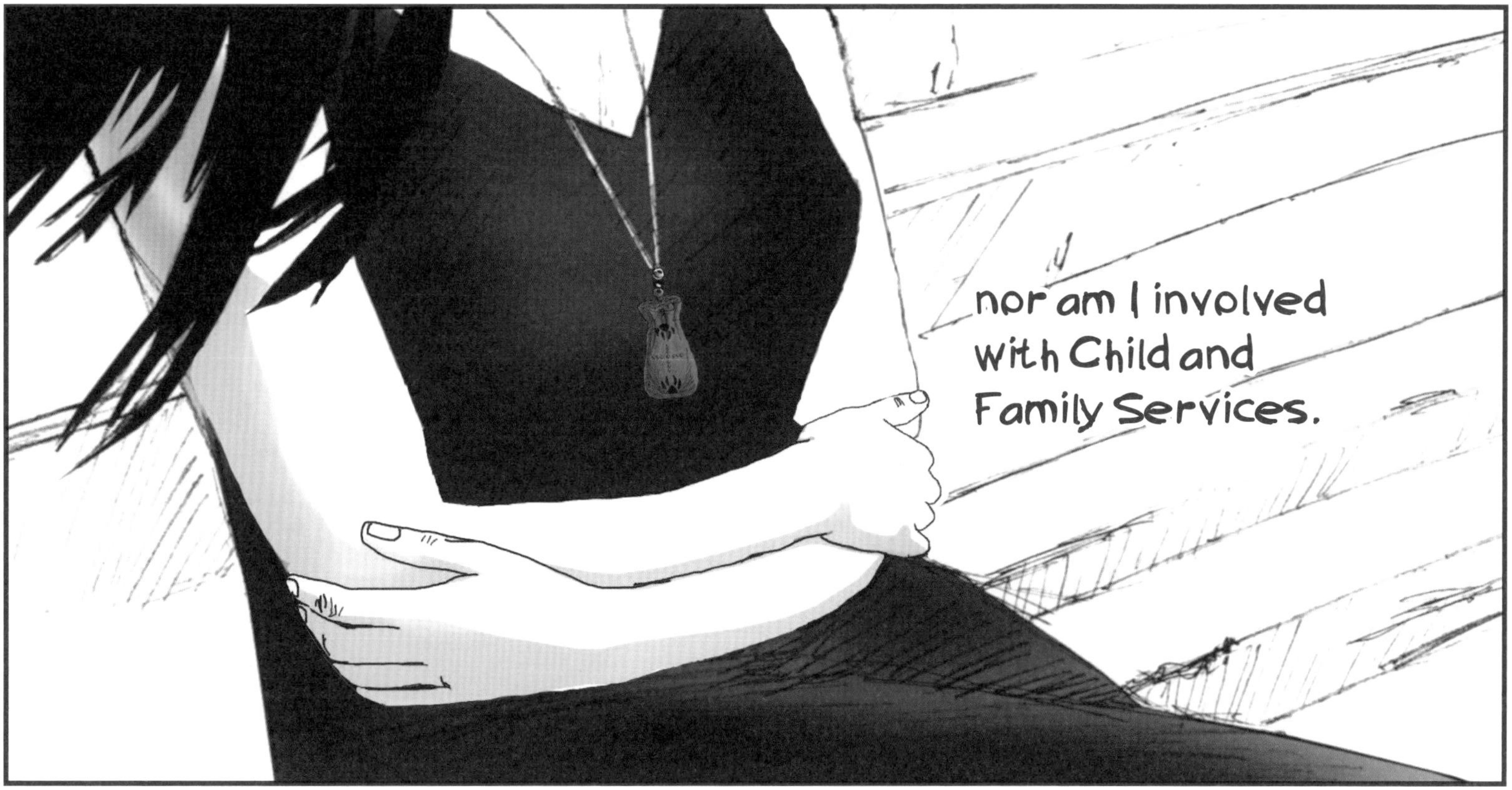
nor am I involved
with Child and
Family Services.

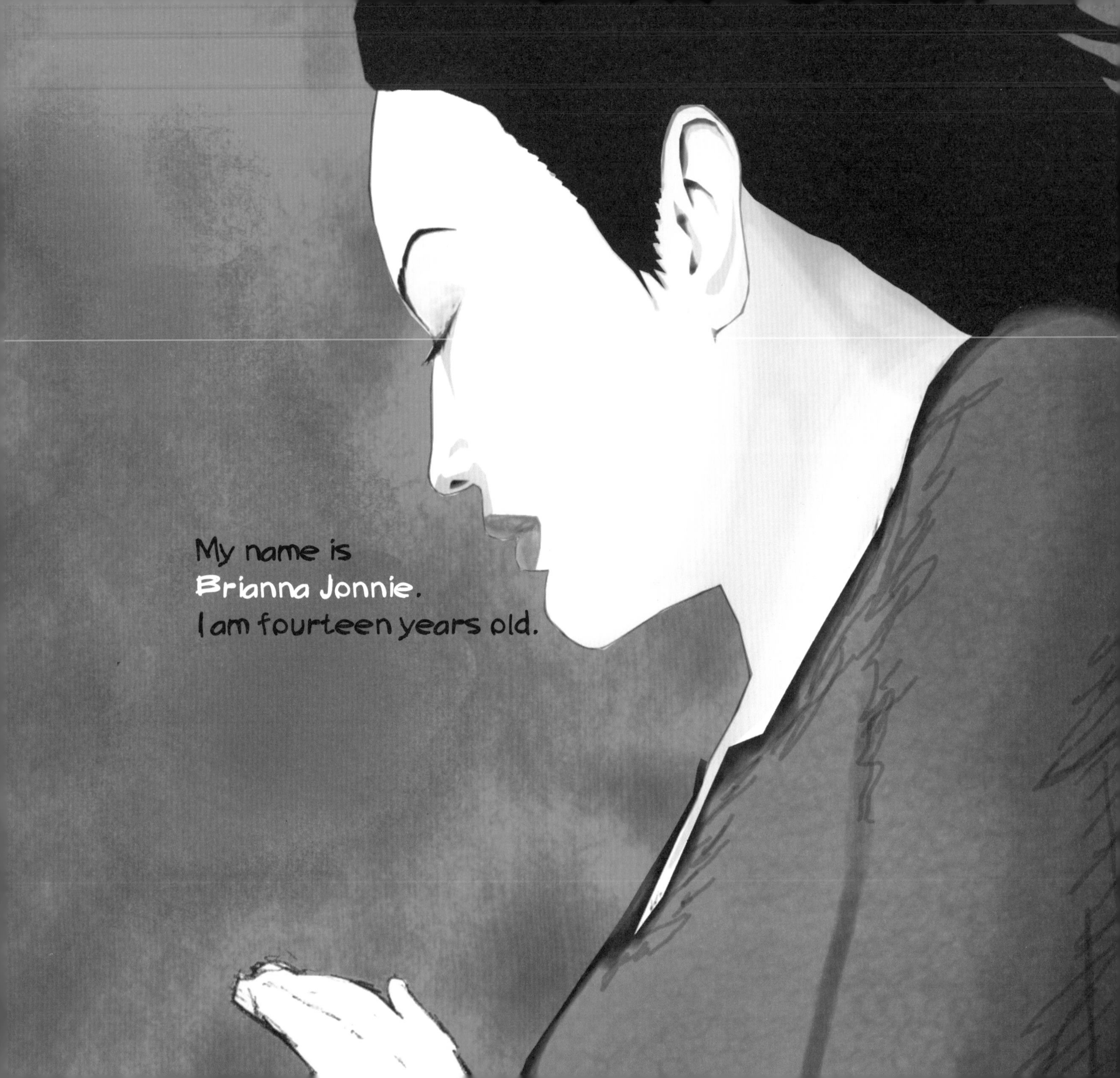

My name is
Brianna Jonnie.
I am fourteen years old.

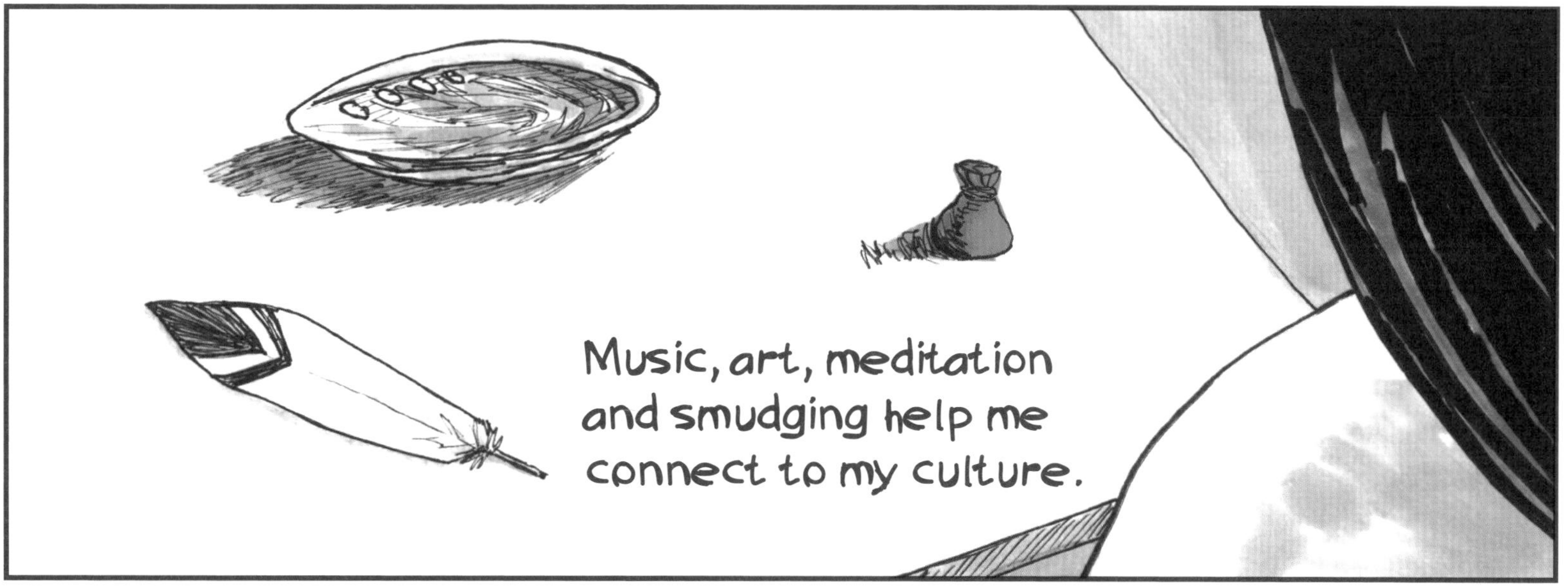
Music, art, meditation
and smudging help me
connect to my culture.

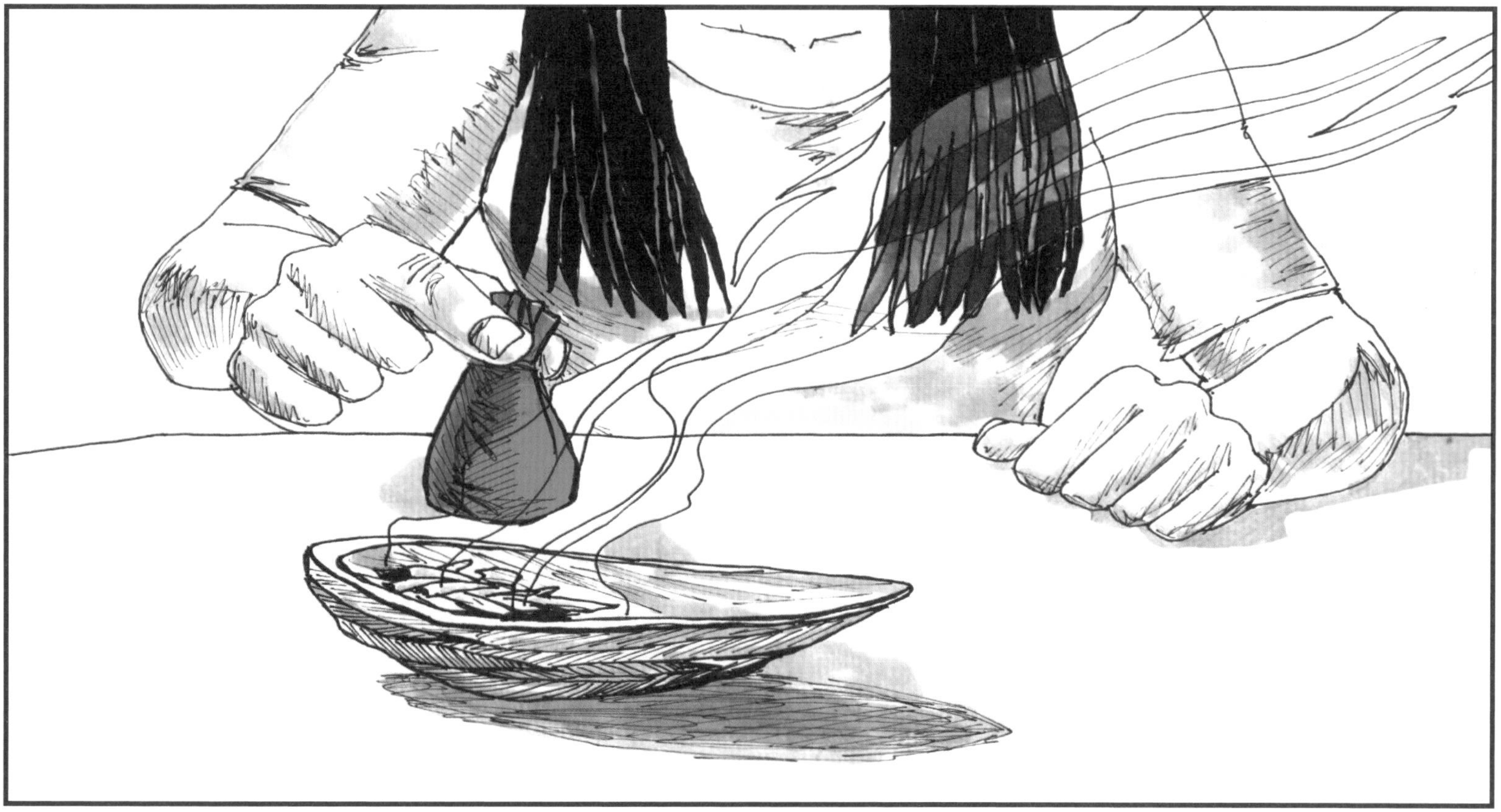

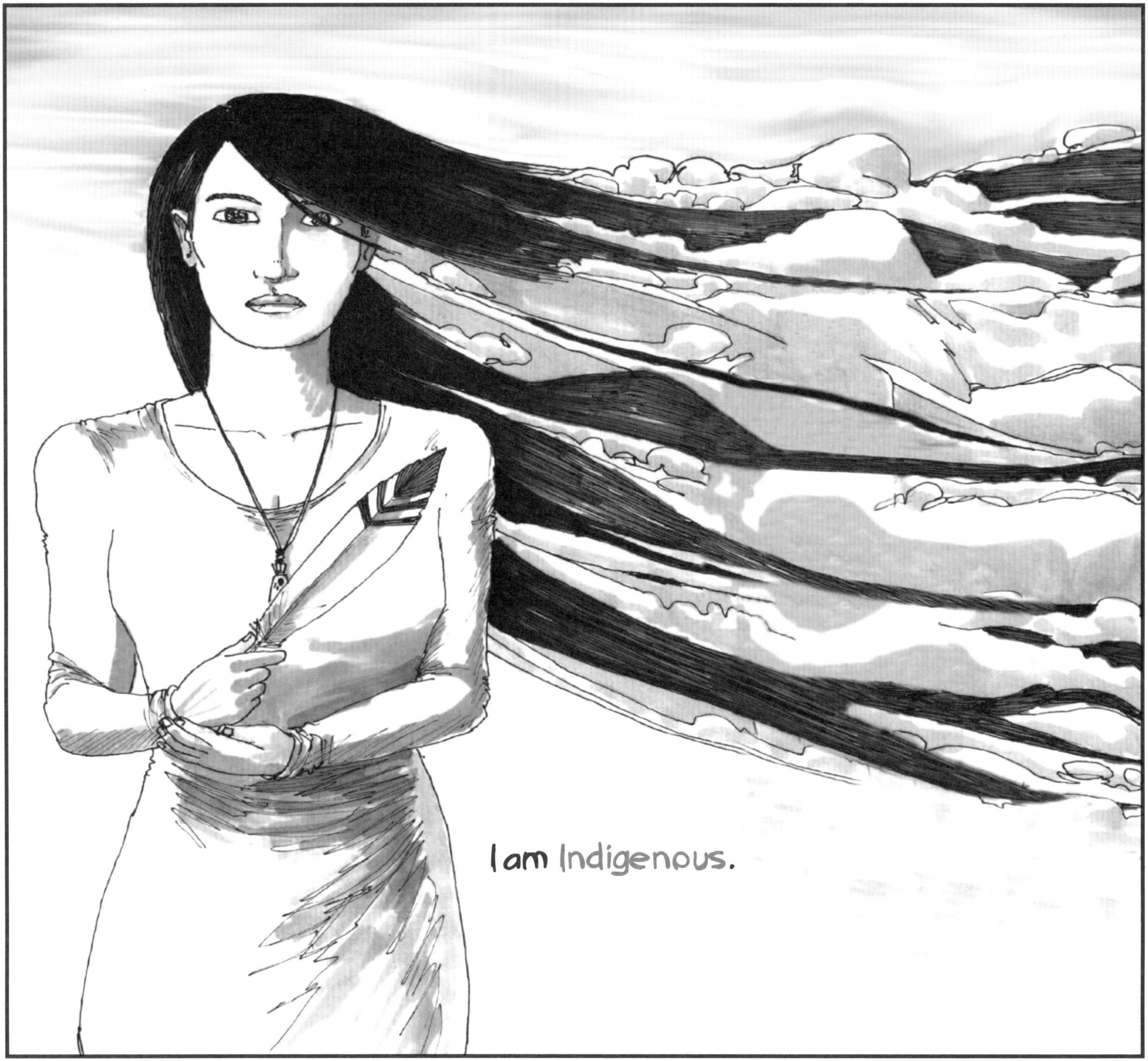
I am Indigenous.

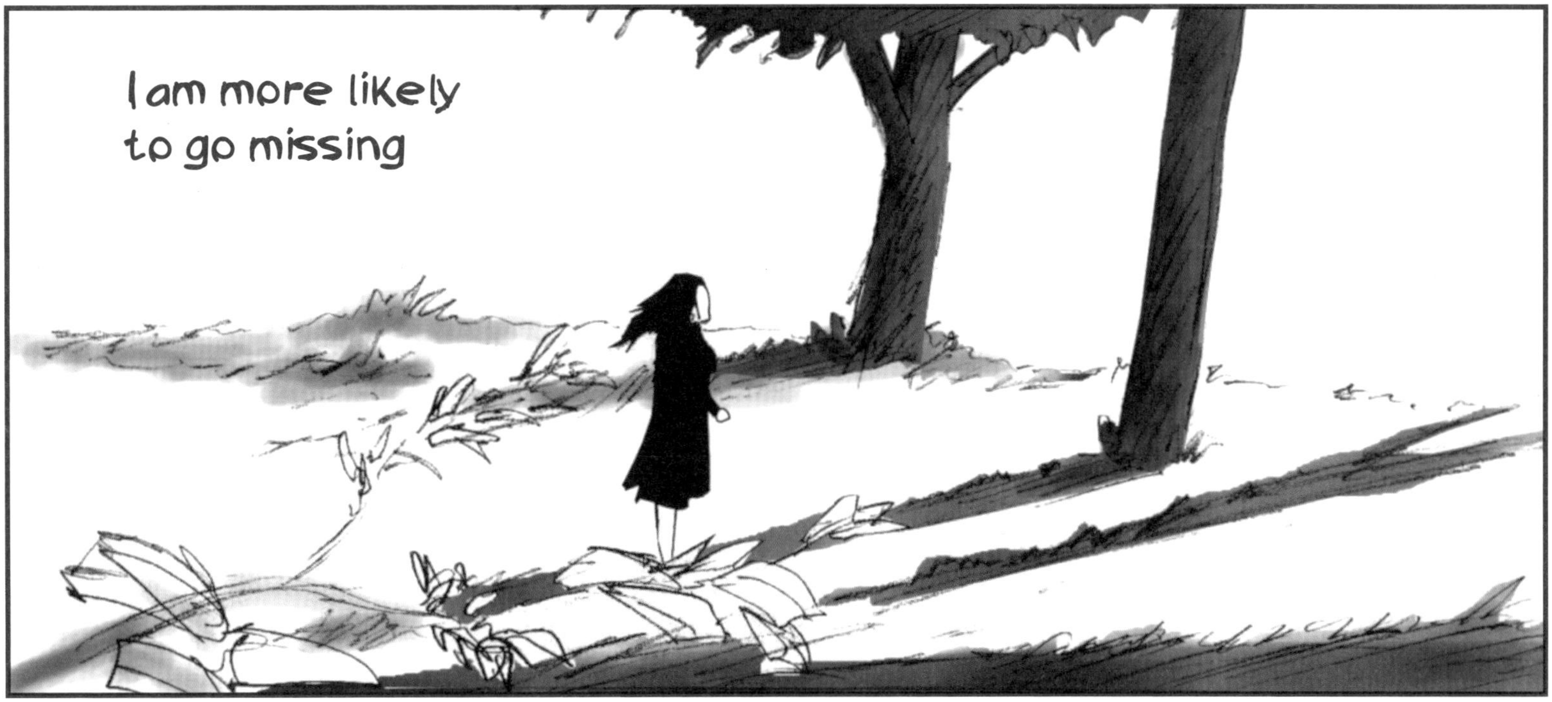
I am more likely
to go missing

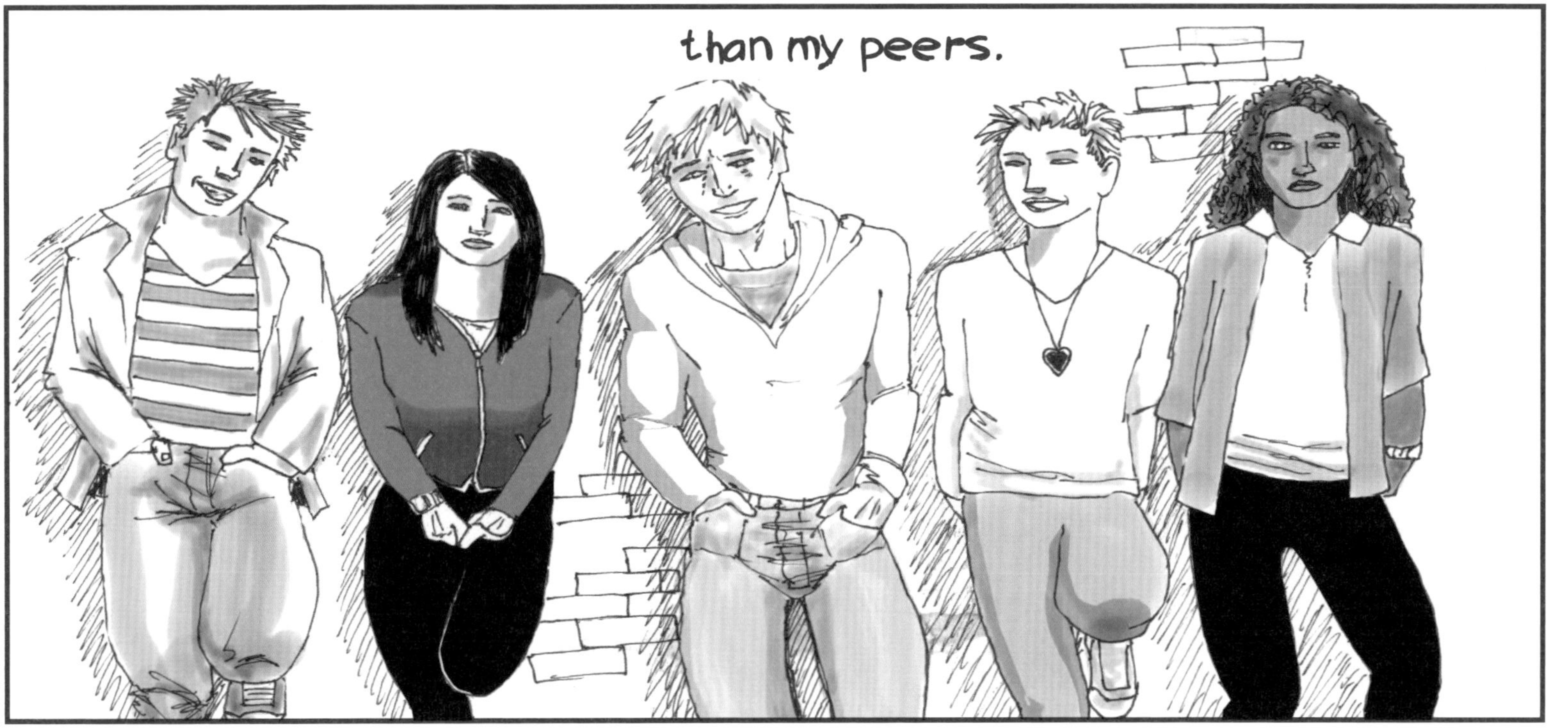
than my peers.

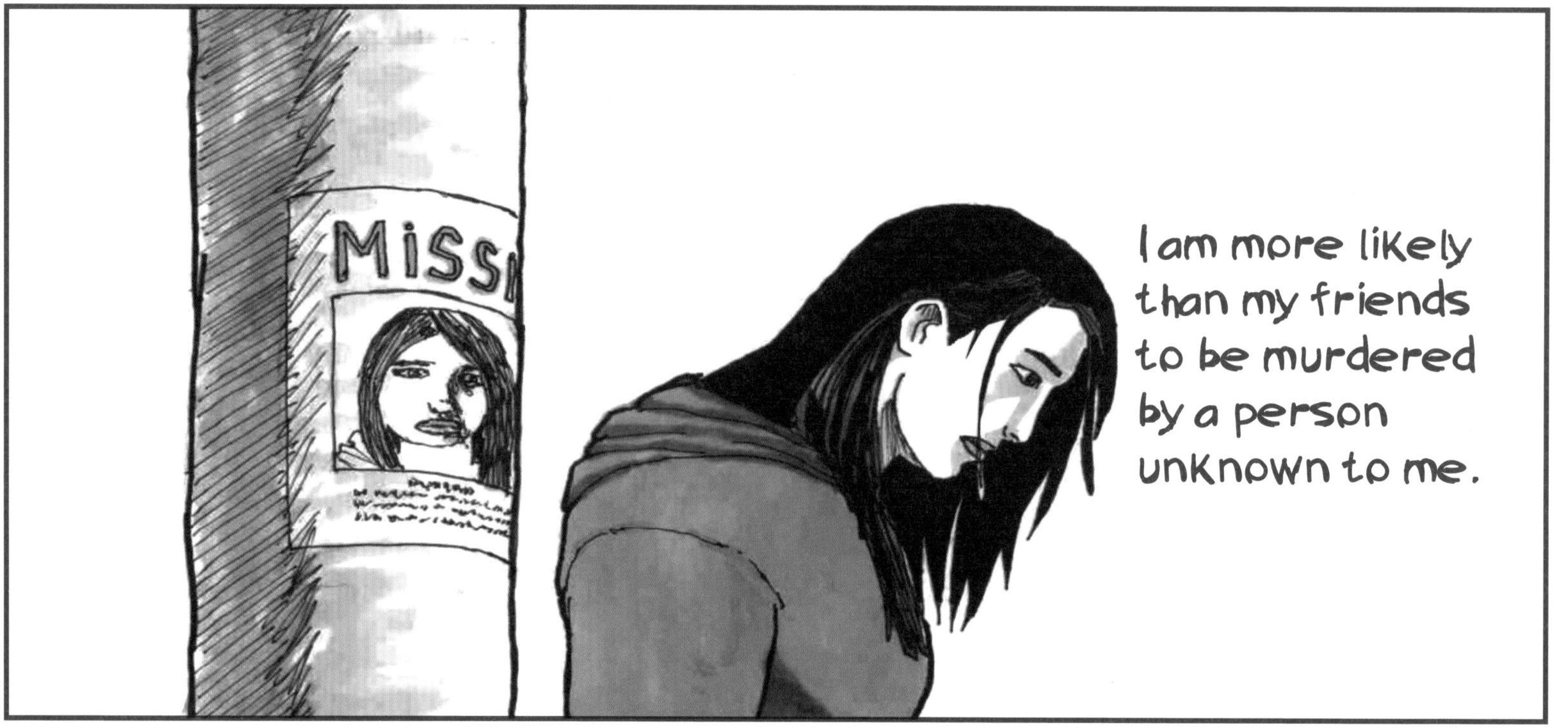
I am more likely
than my friends
to be murdered
by a person
unknown to me.

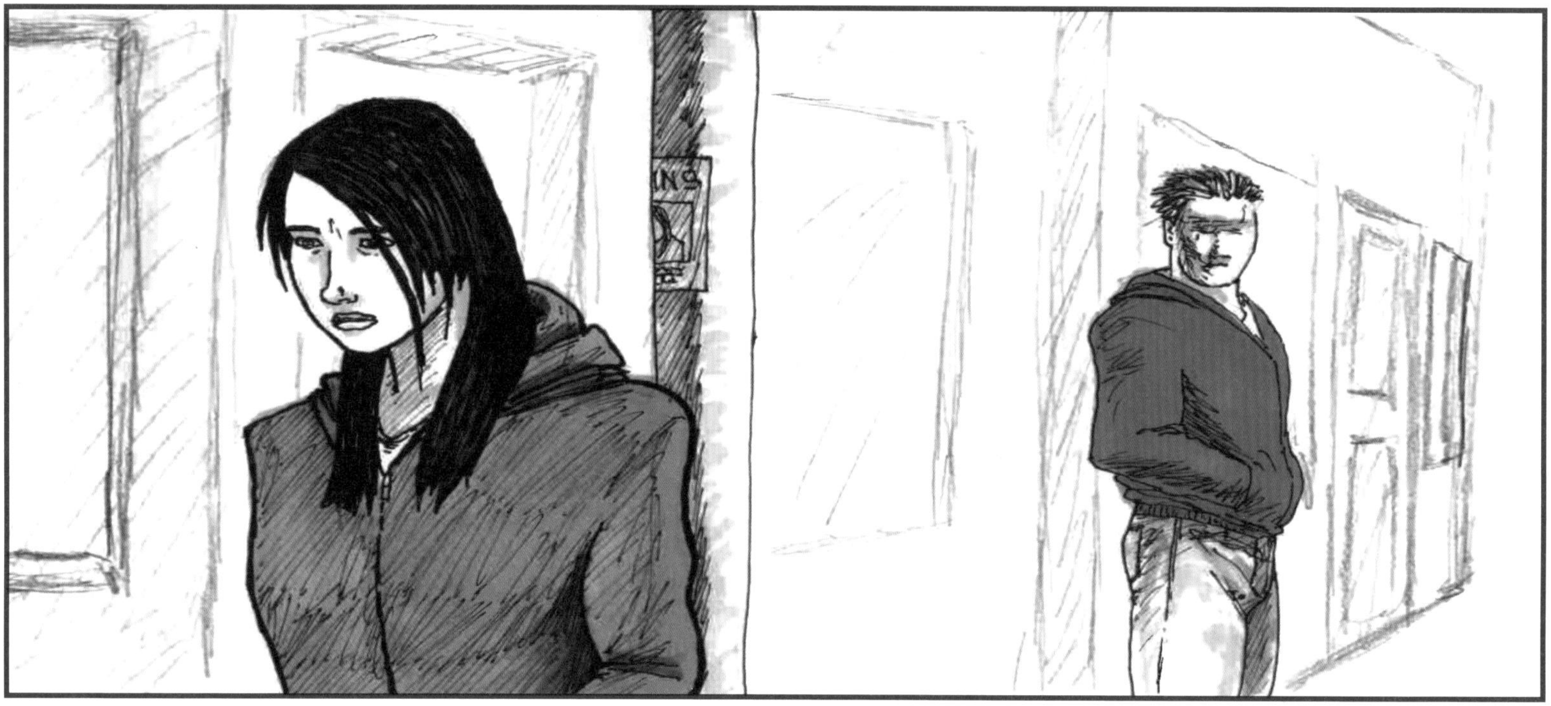

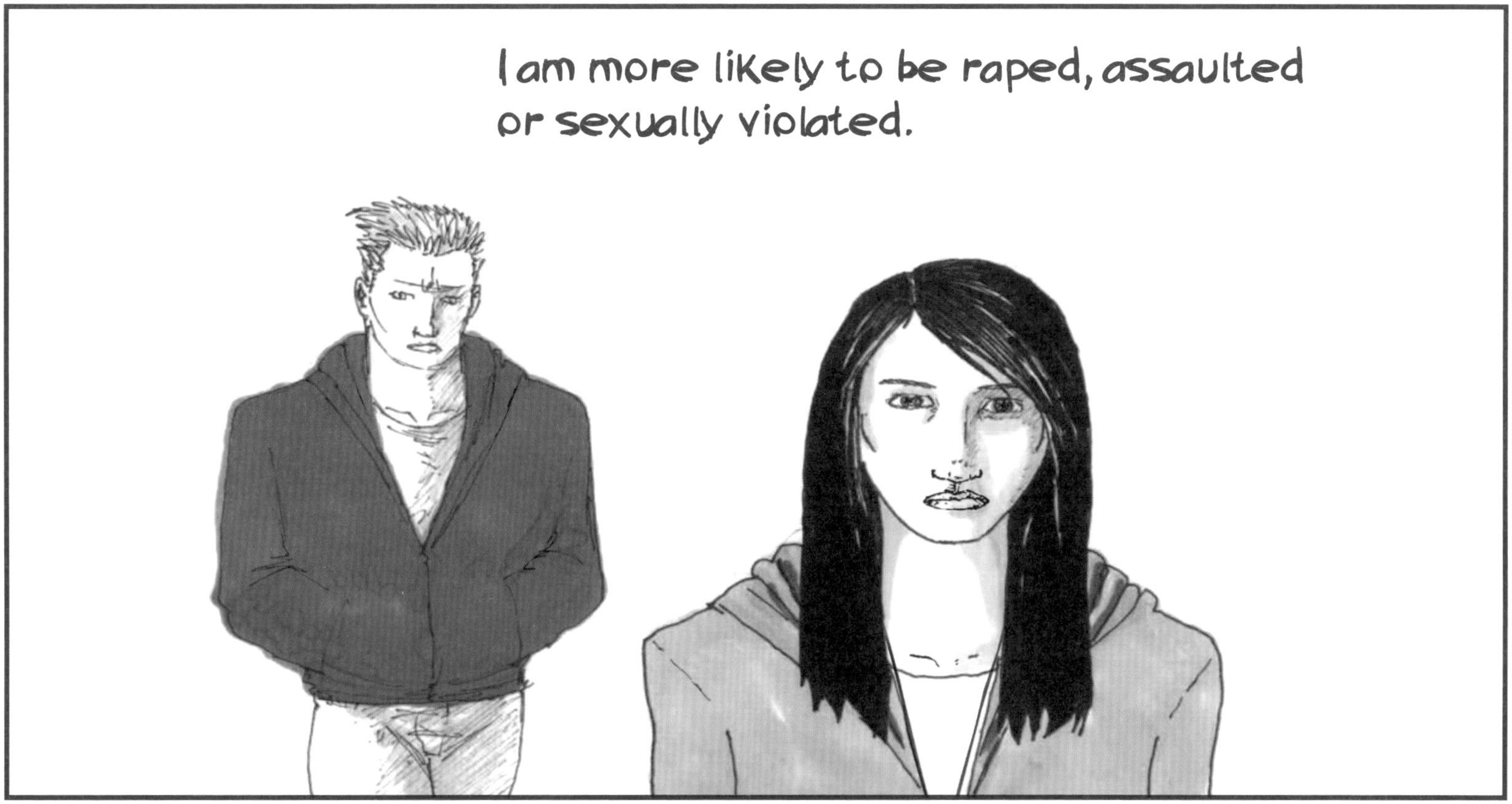
I am more likely to be raped, assaulted
or sexually violated.

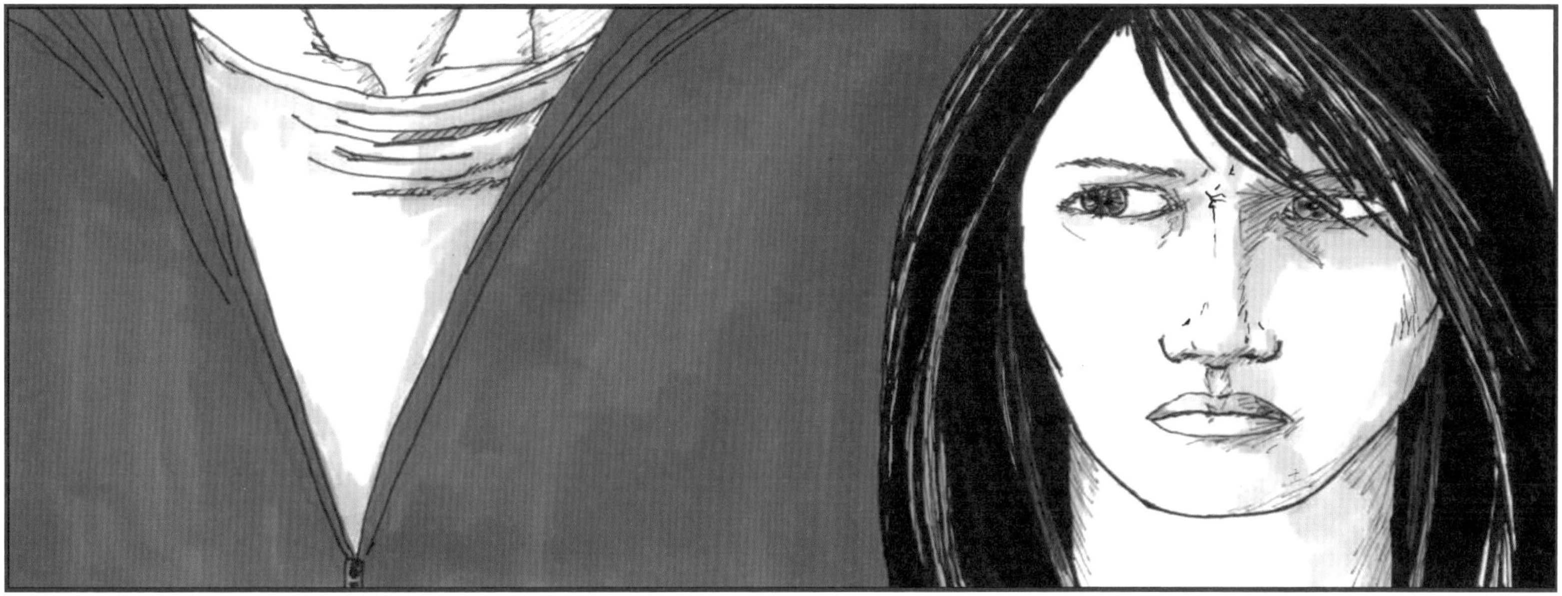

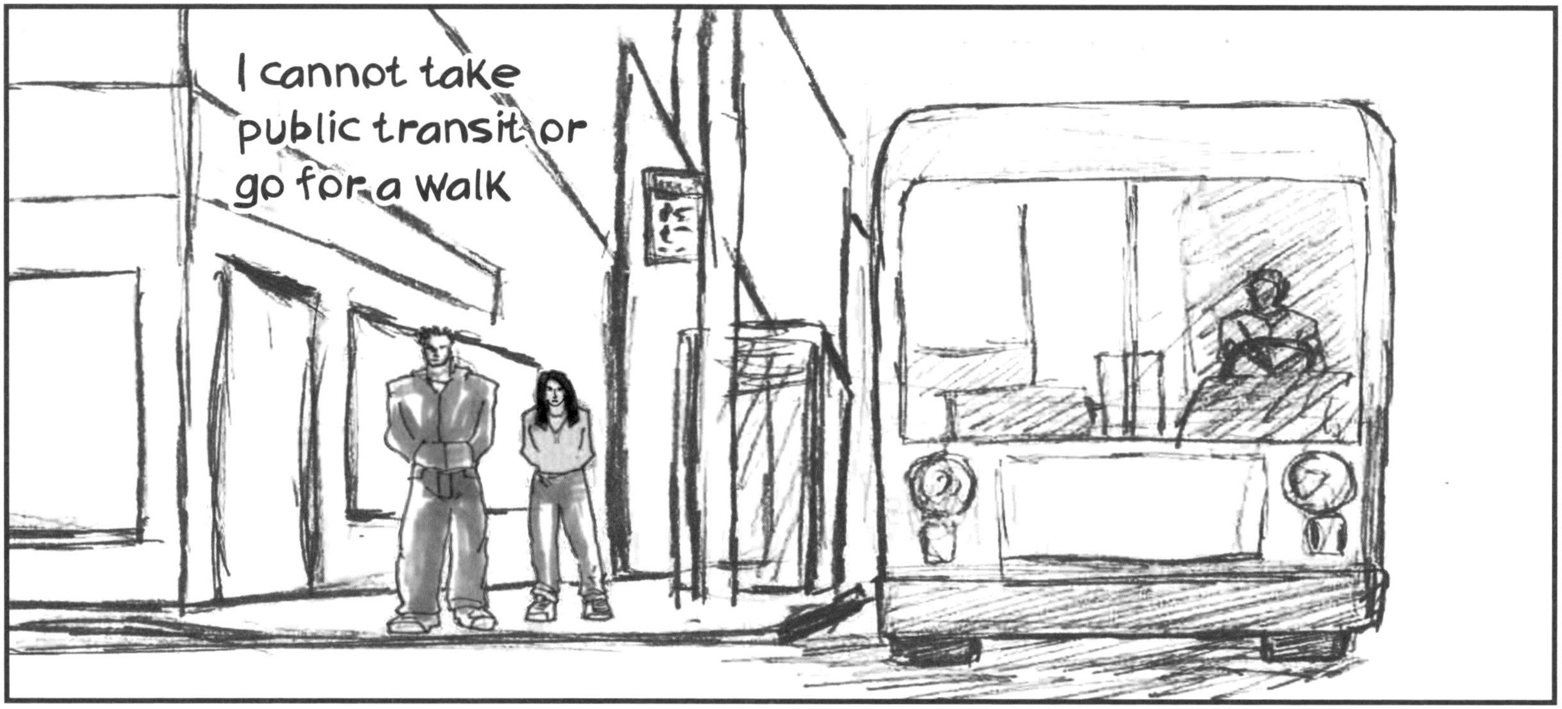
I cannot take
public transit or
go for a walk

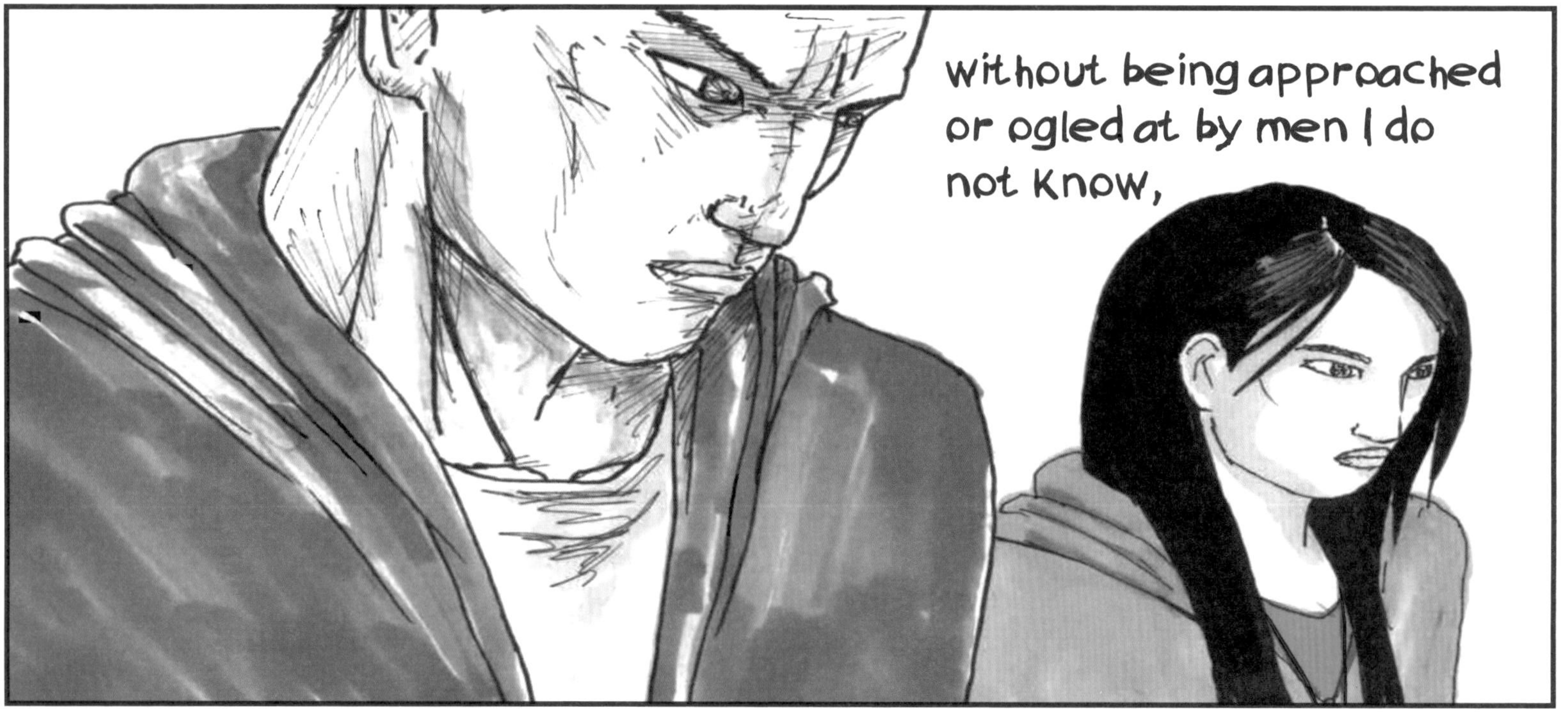
without being approached
or ogled at by men I do
not know,

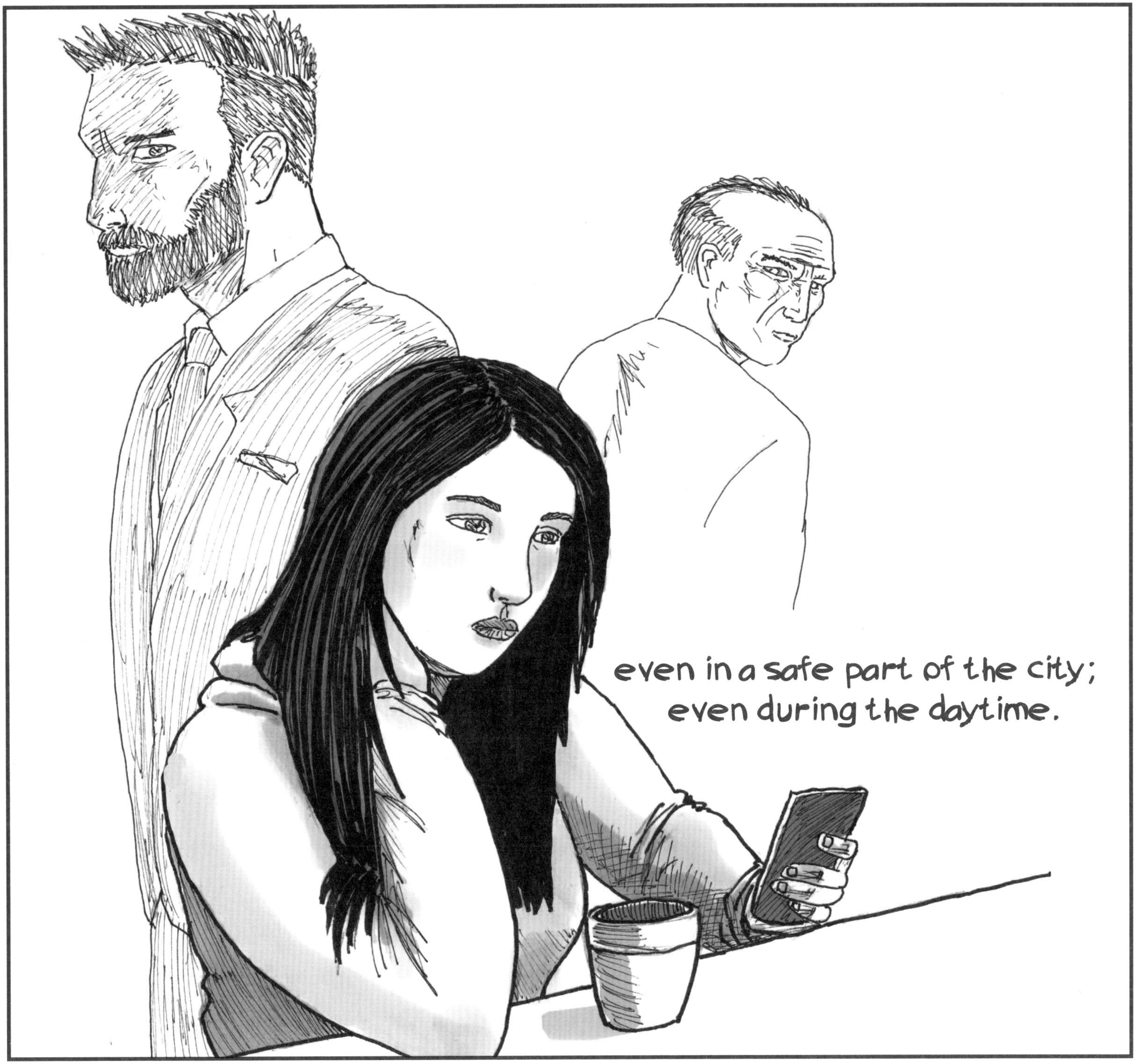
even in a safe part of the city;
even during the daytime.

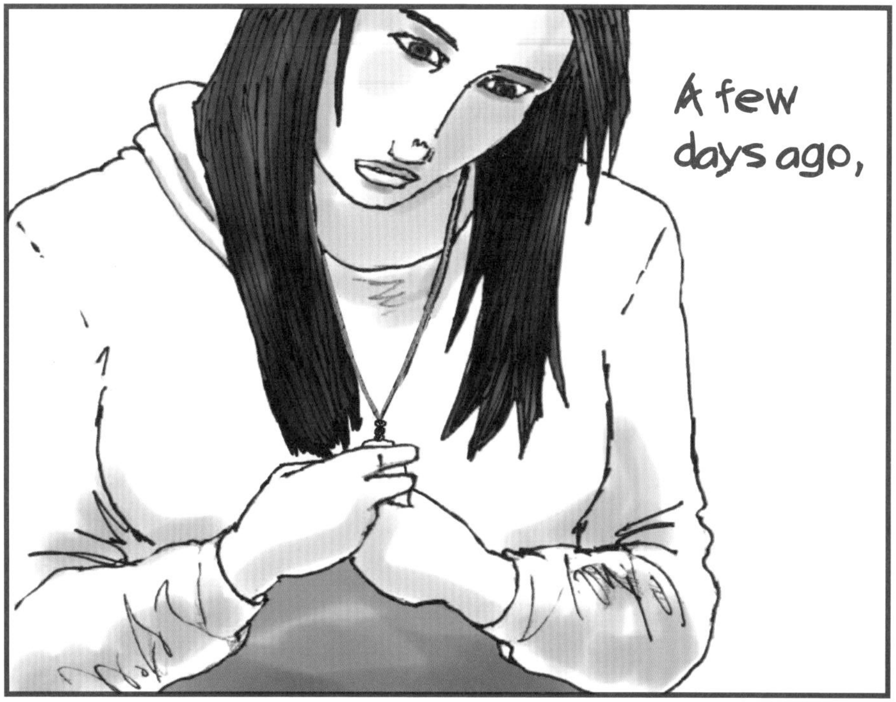
A few
days ago,

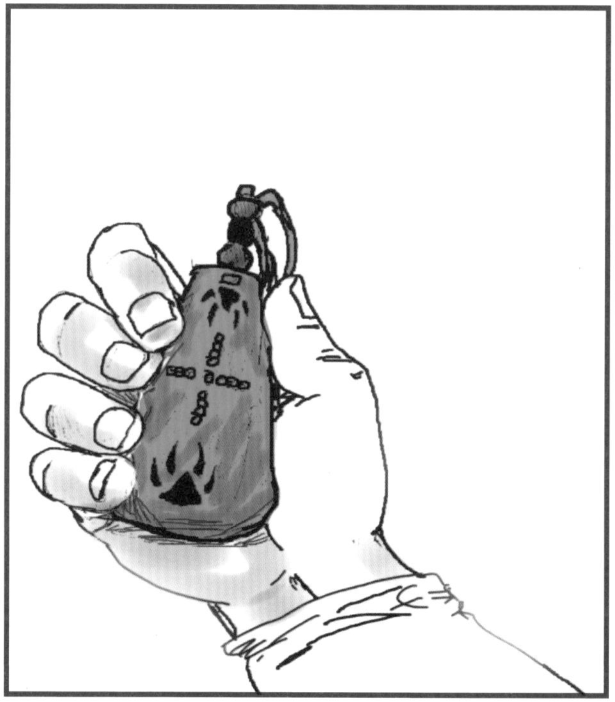

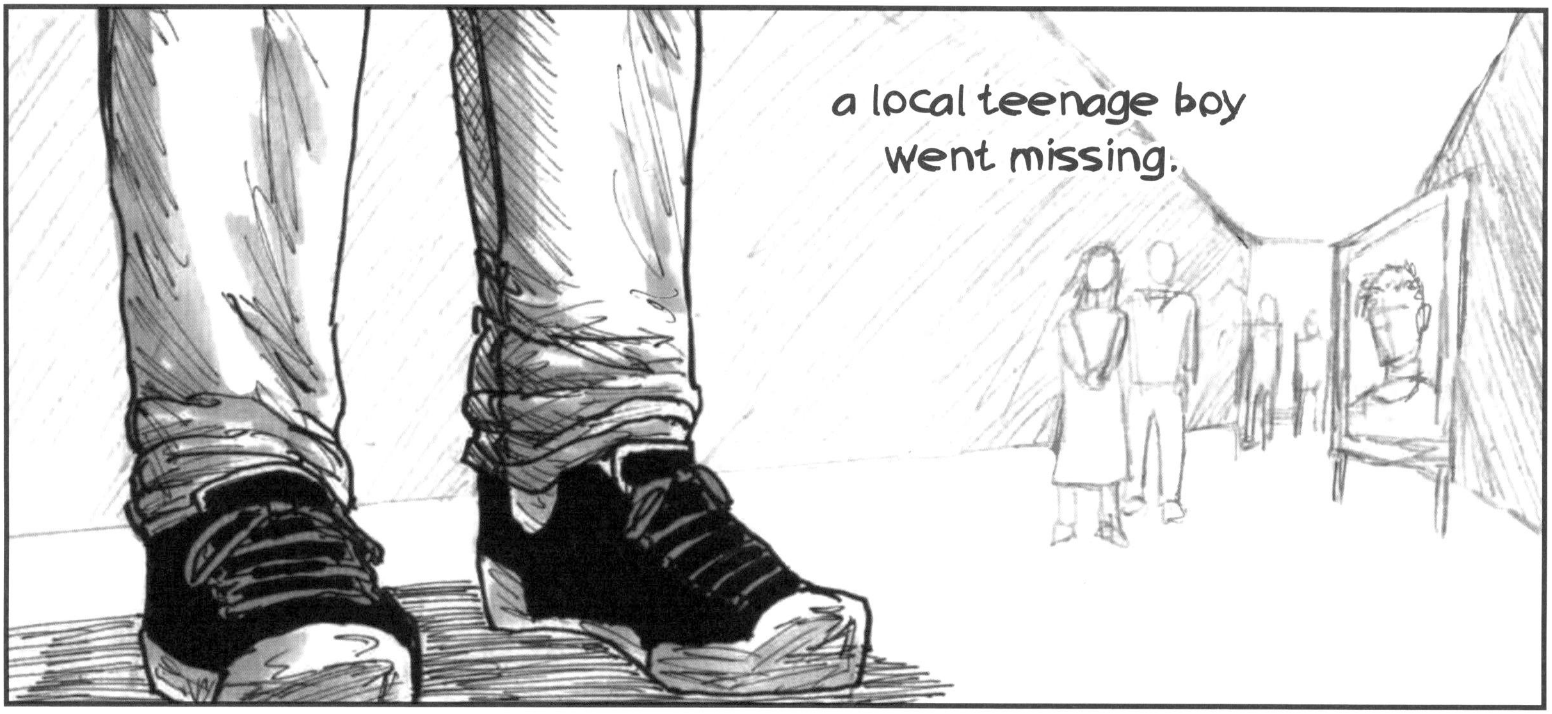
a local teenage boy
went missing.

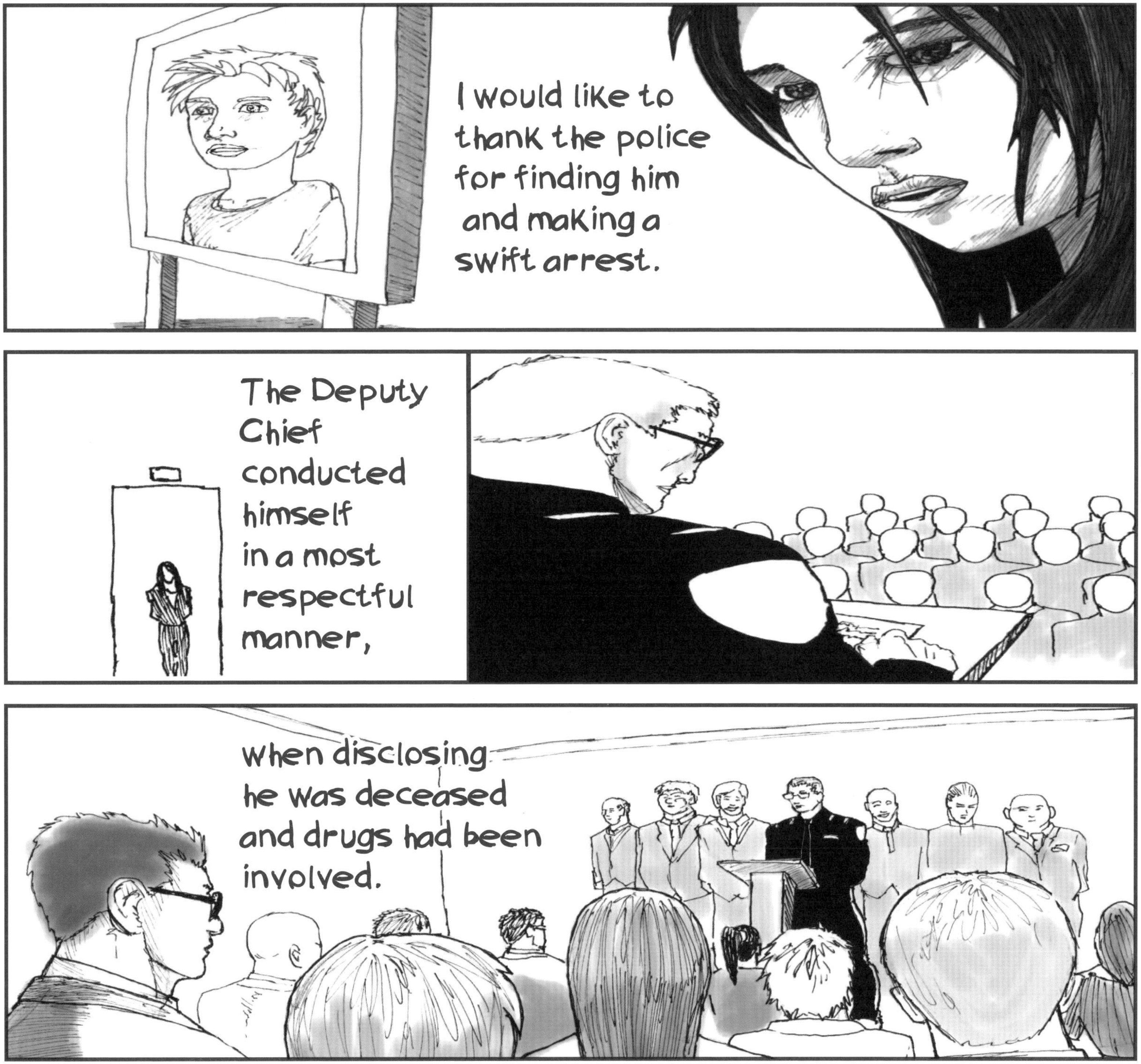
I would like to thank the police for finding him and making a swift arrest.
The Deputy Chief conducted himself in a most respectful manner,
when disclosing he was deceased and drugs had been involved.

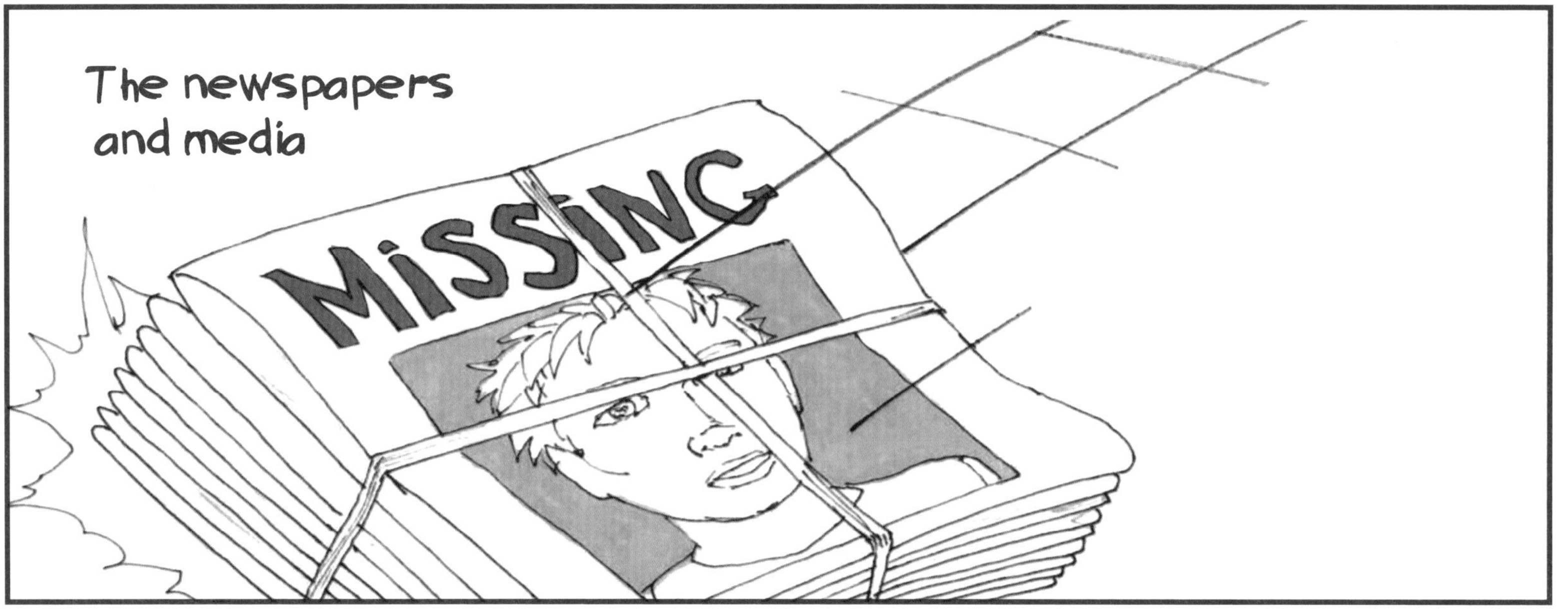
The newspapers and media
MISSING

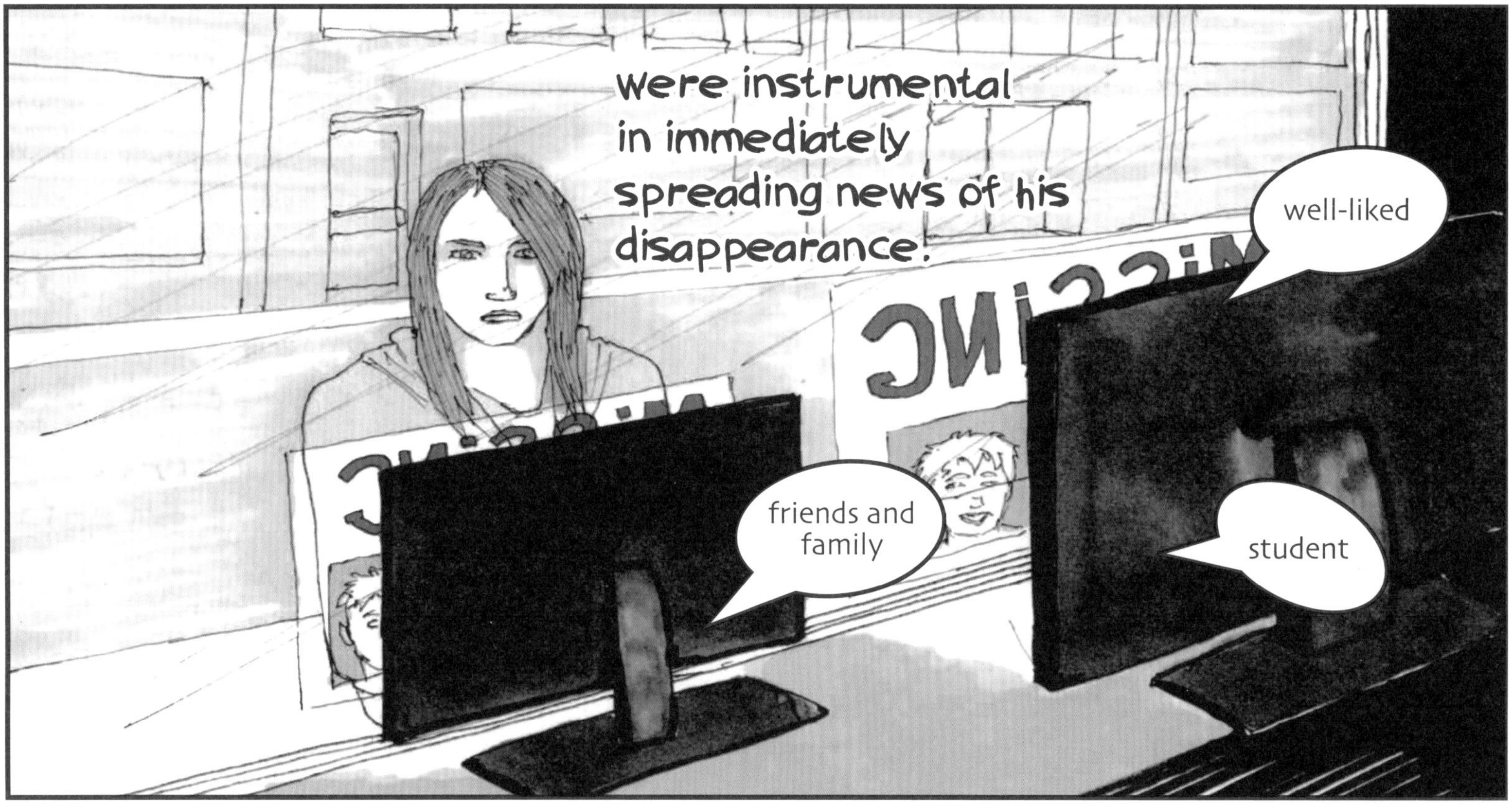
were instrumental in immediately spreading news of his disappearance.
well-liked
friends and family
student

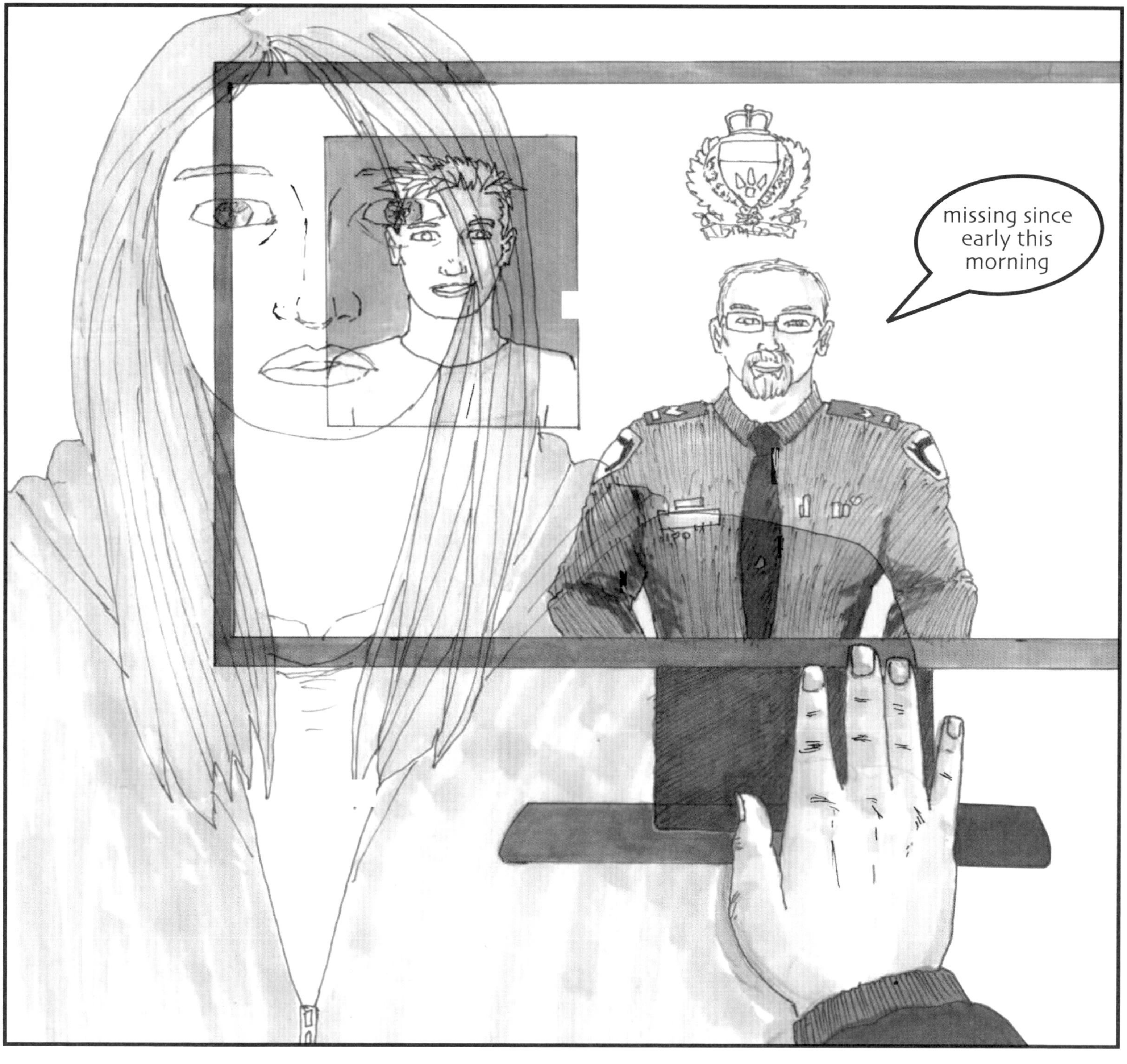
missing since early this morning

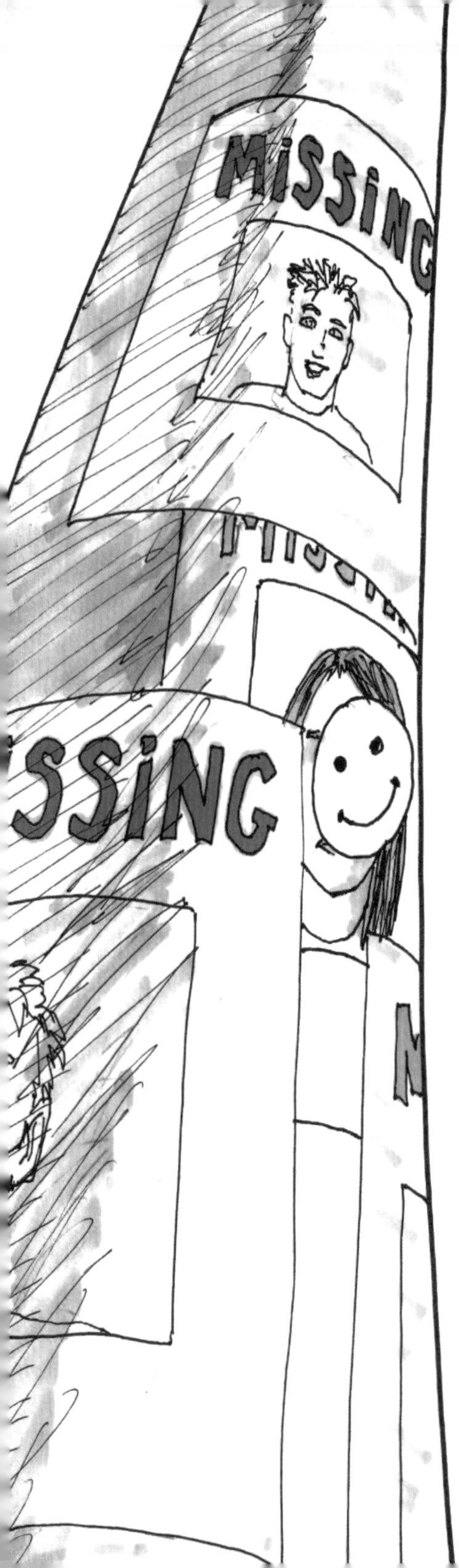
MISSING
SSING

I have noticed that missing Indigenous girls are not afforded the same courtesies by the community, the media or the police.

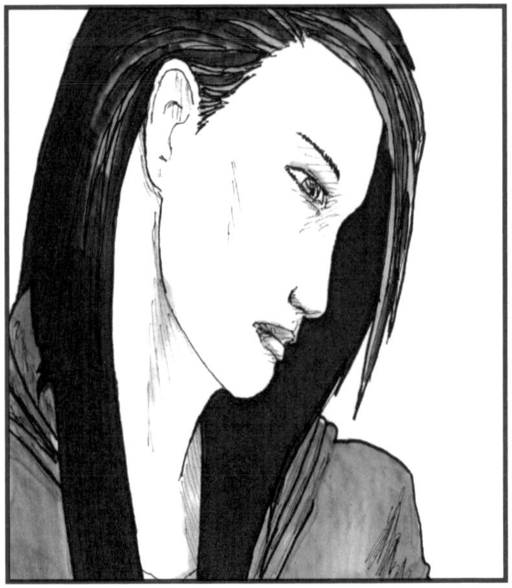

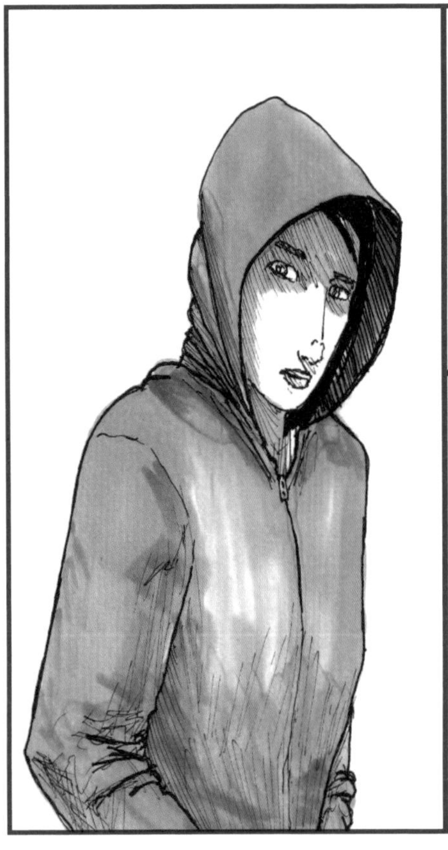

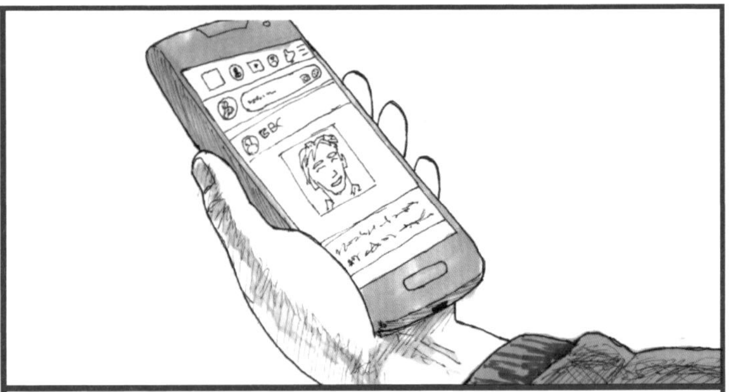

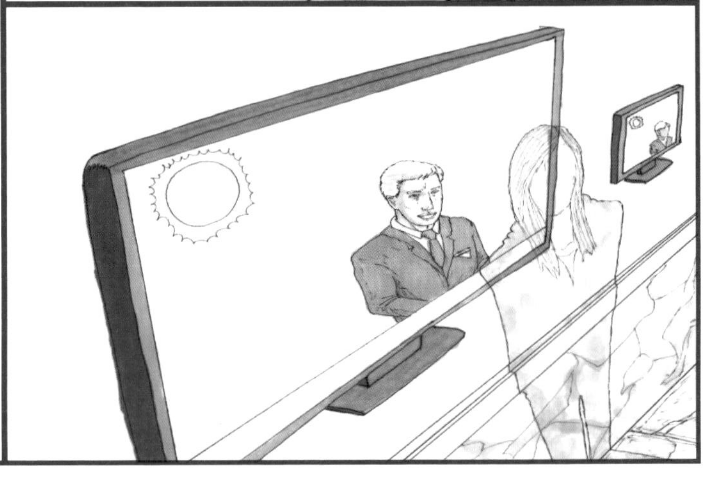

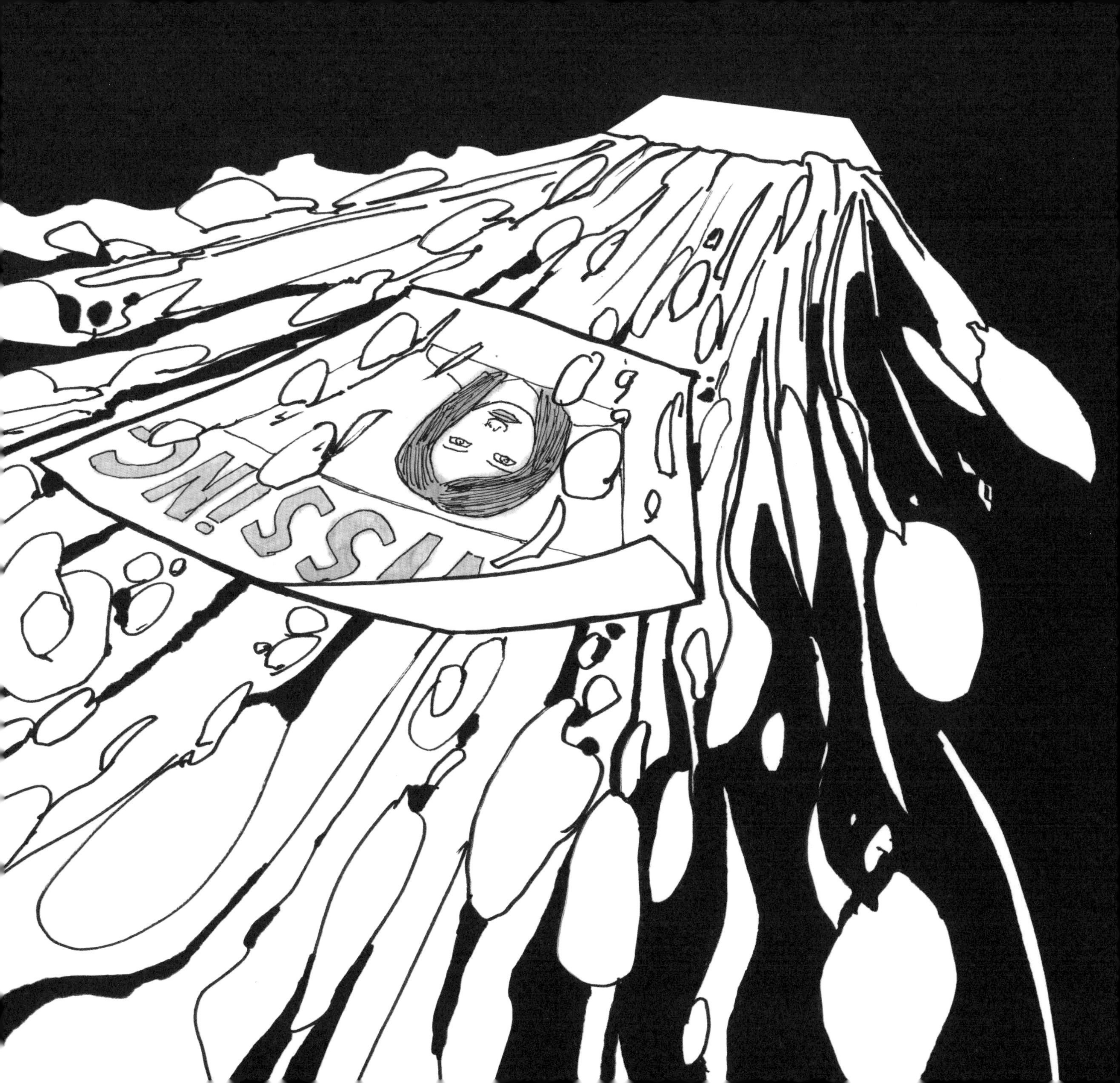

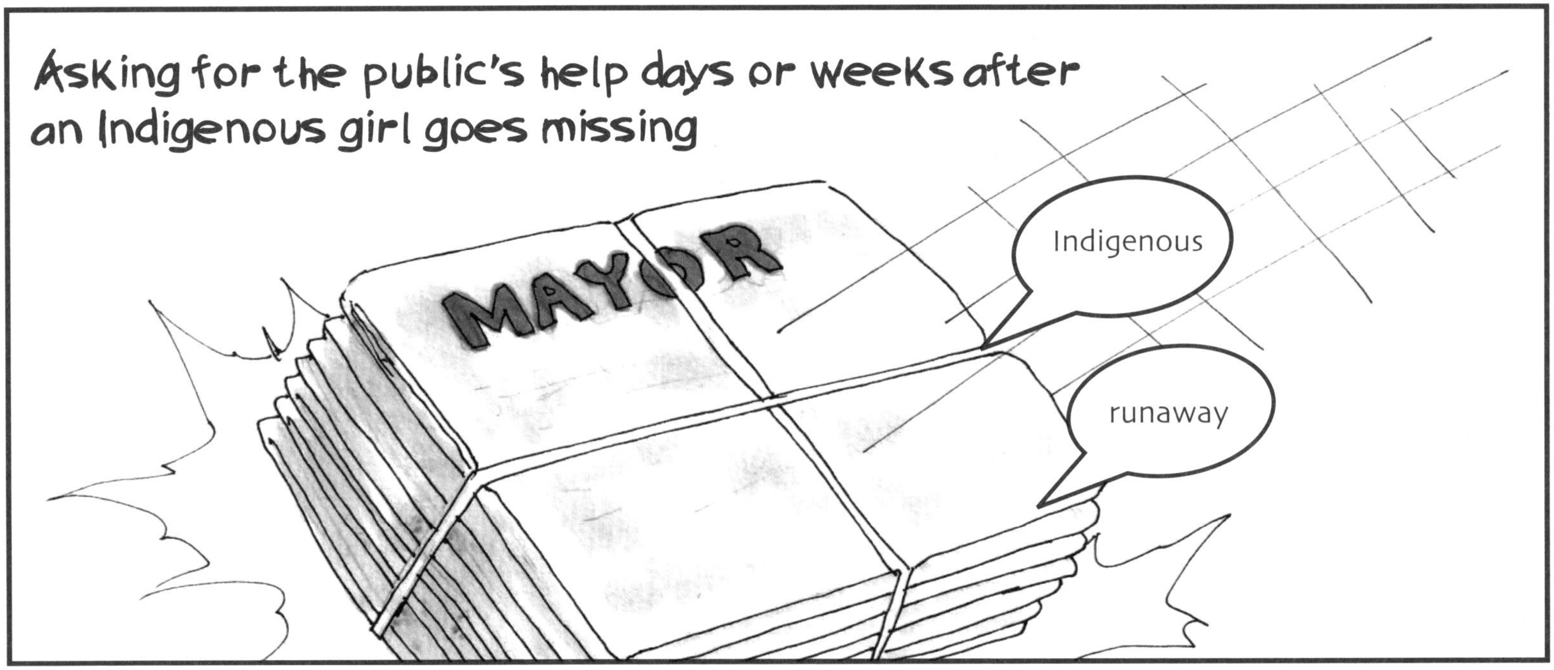
Asking for the public's help days or weeks after an Indigenous girl goes missing
MAYOR
Indigenous
runaway

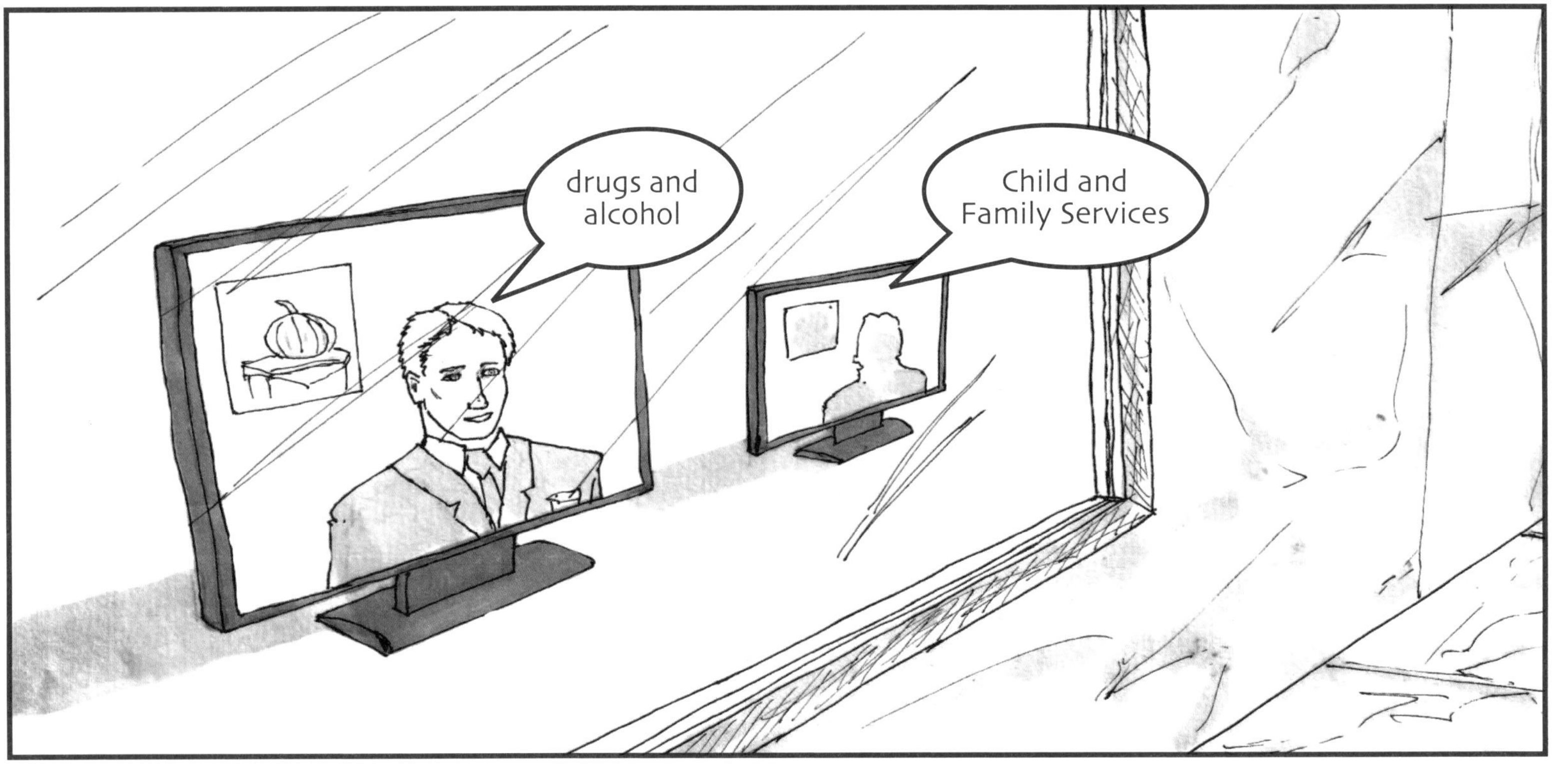
drugs and alcohol
Child and Family Services

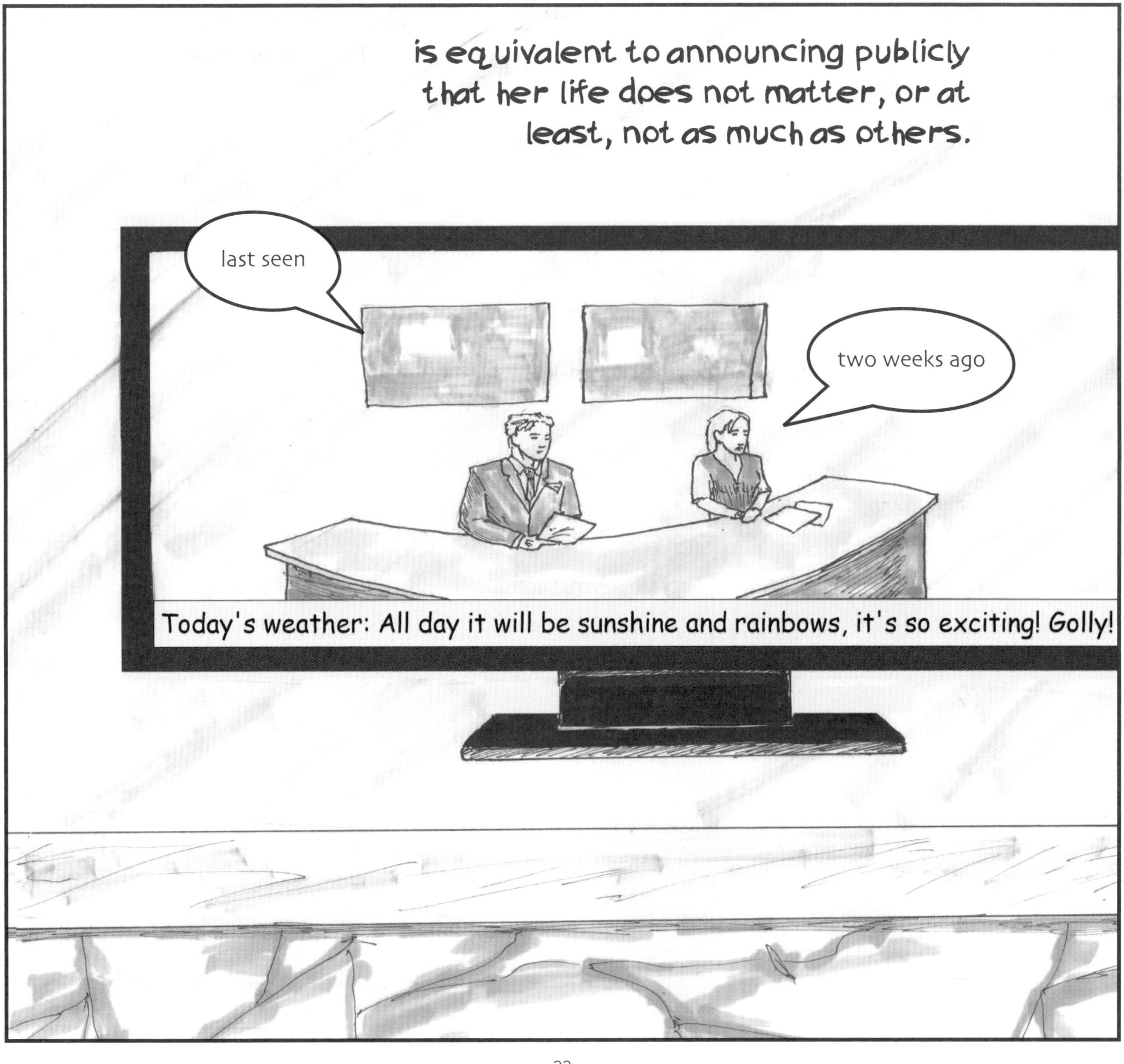
is equivalent to announcing publicly that her life does not matter, or at least, not as much as others.
last seen
two weeks ago
Today's weather: All day it will be sunshine and rainbows, it's so exciting! Golly!

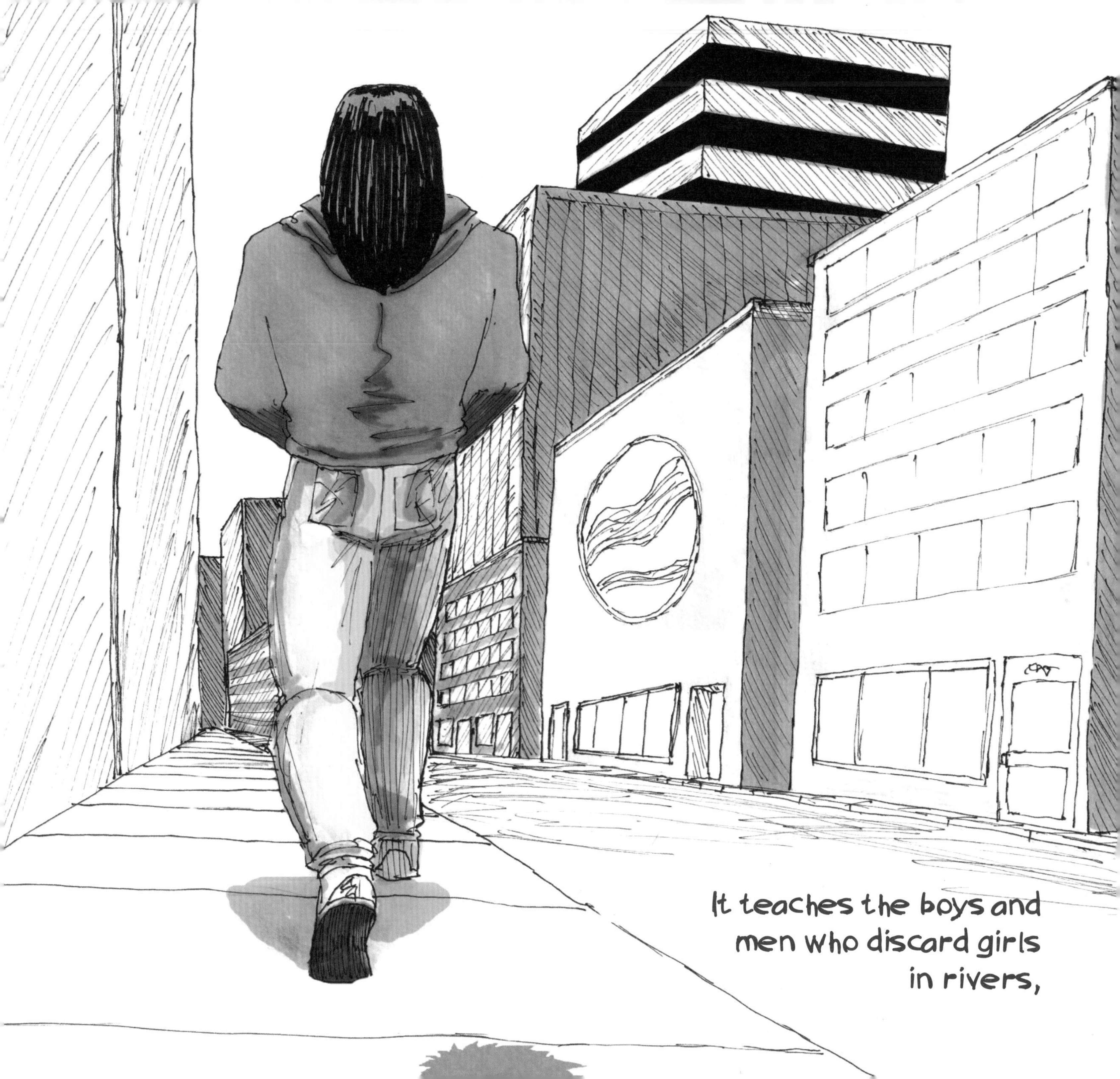

It teaches the boys and men who discard girls in rivers,

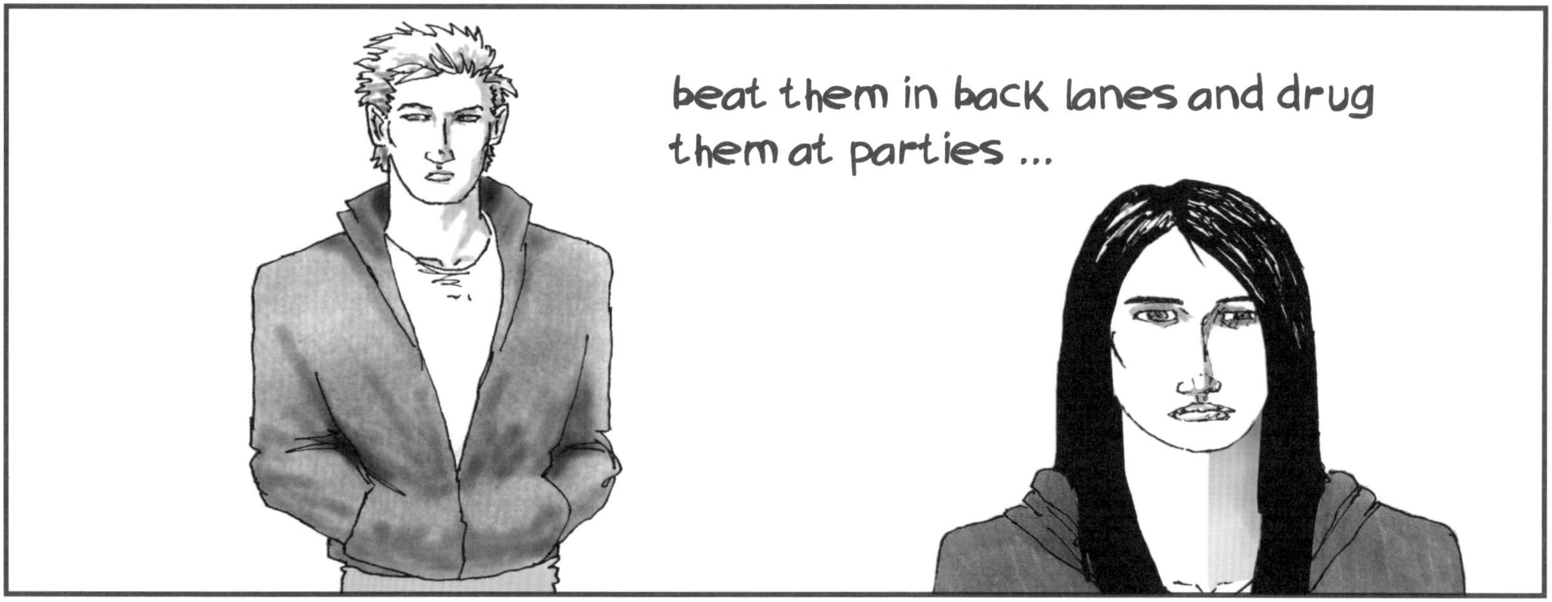
beat them in back lanes and drug them at parties ...

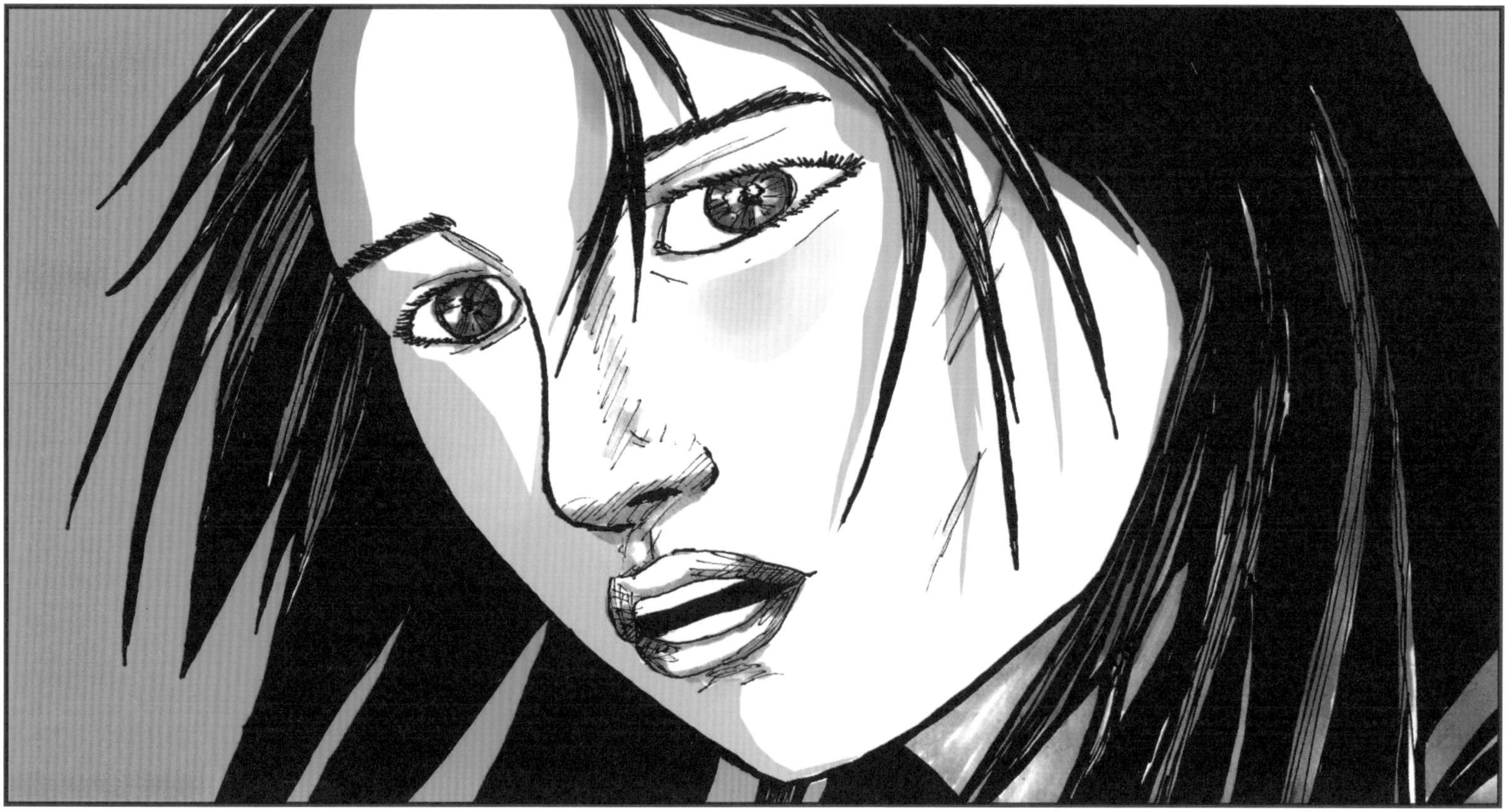

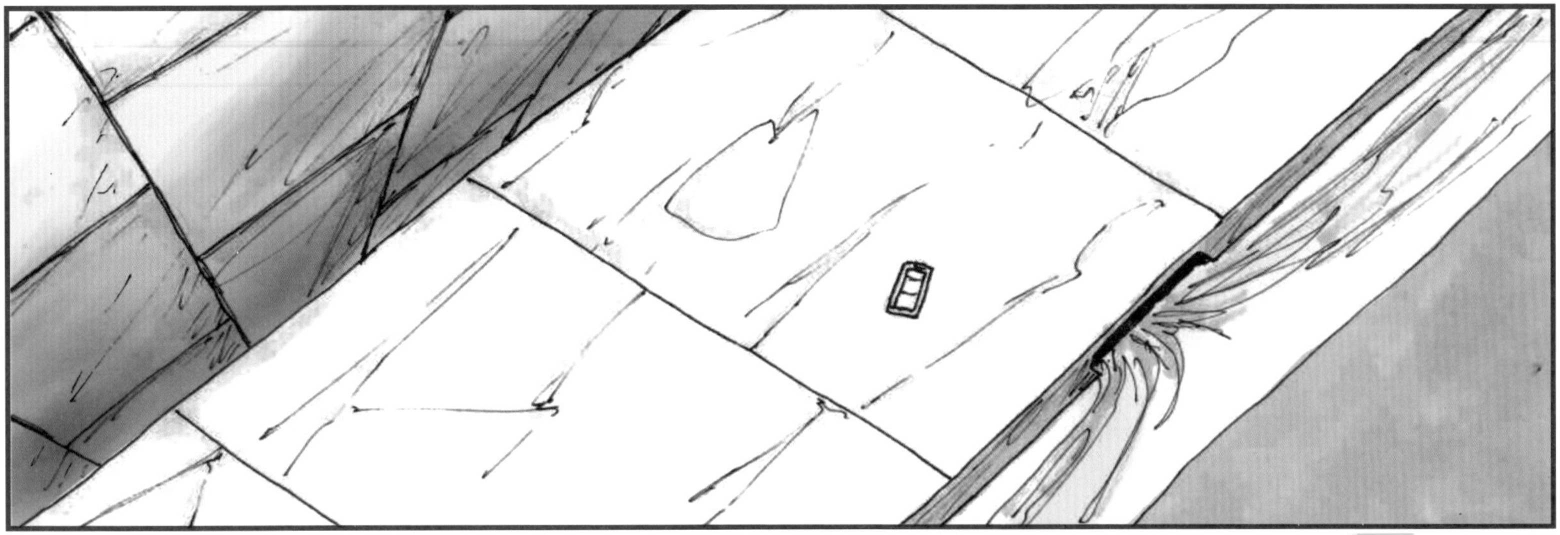

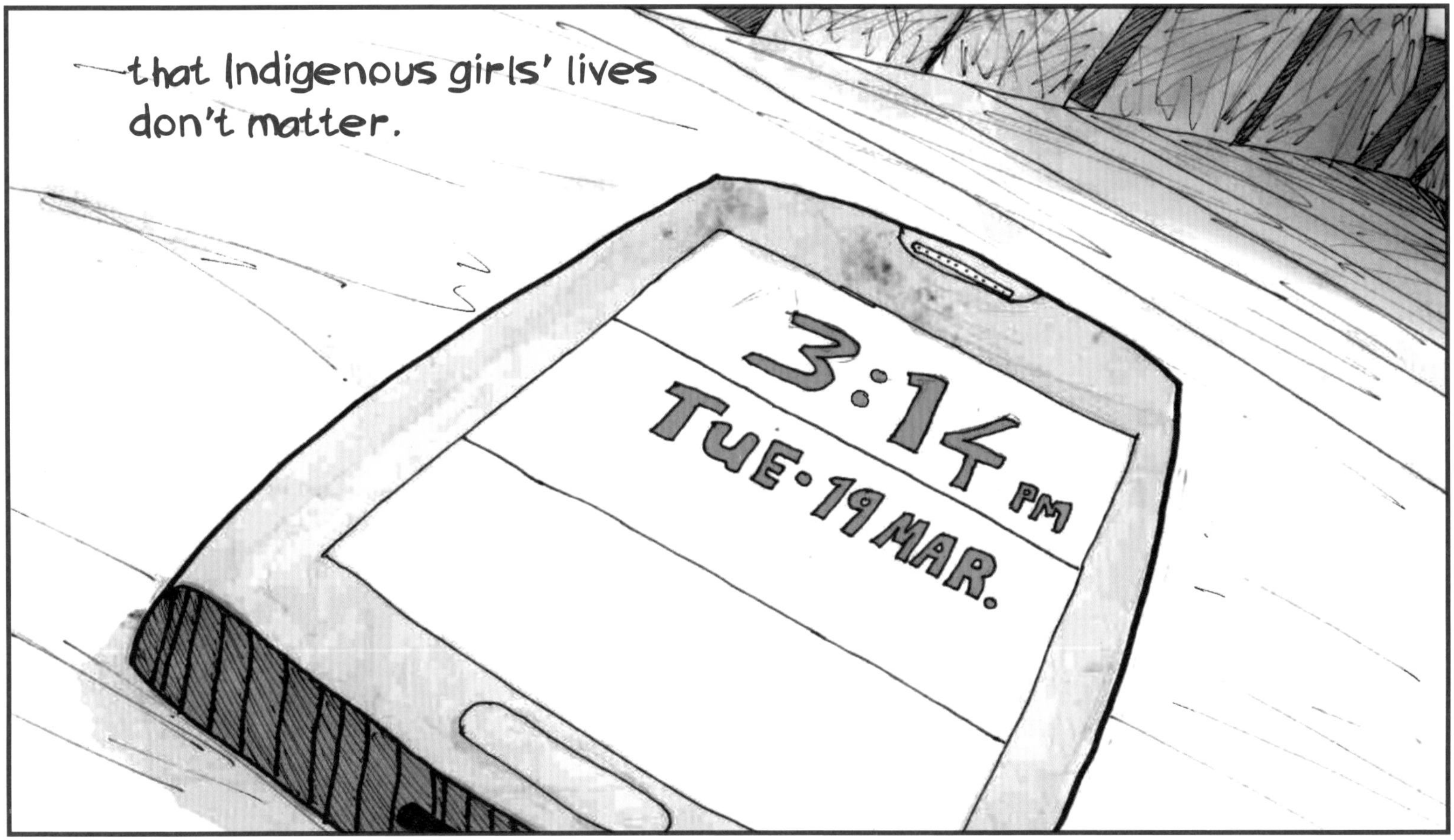
—that Indigenous girls' lives don't matter.
3:14 PM
TUE • 19 MAR.

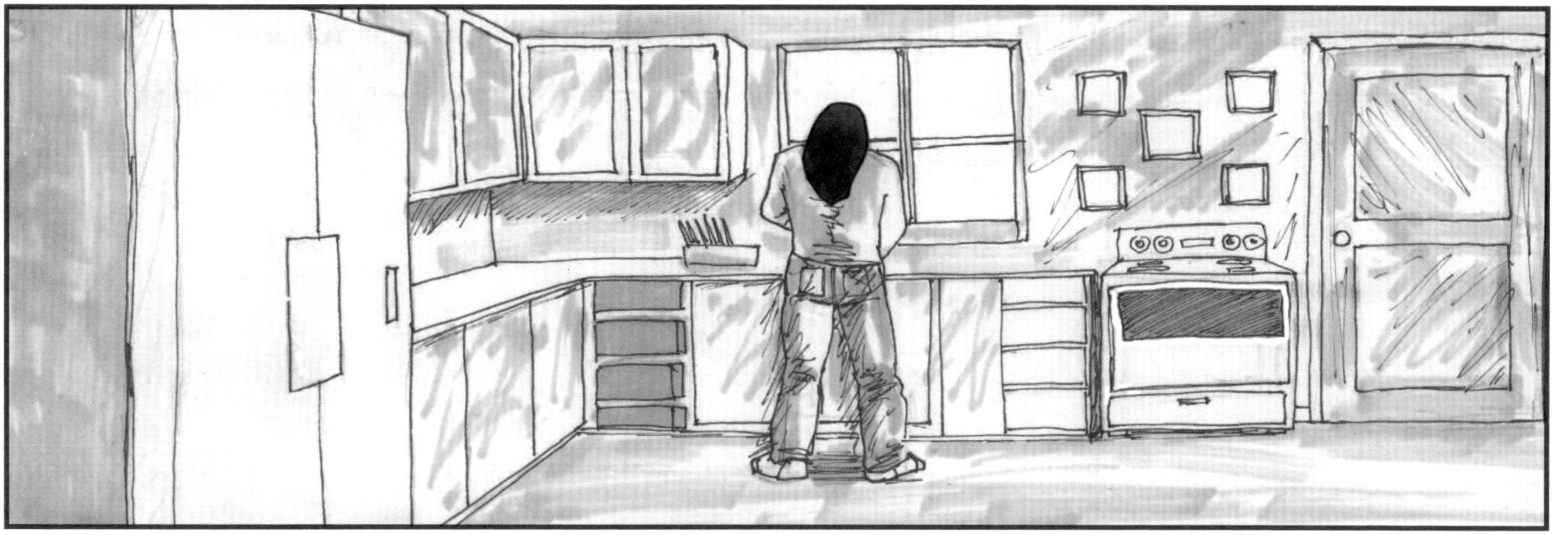

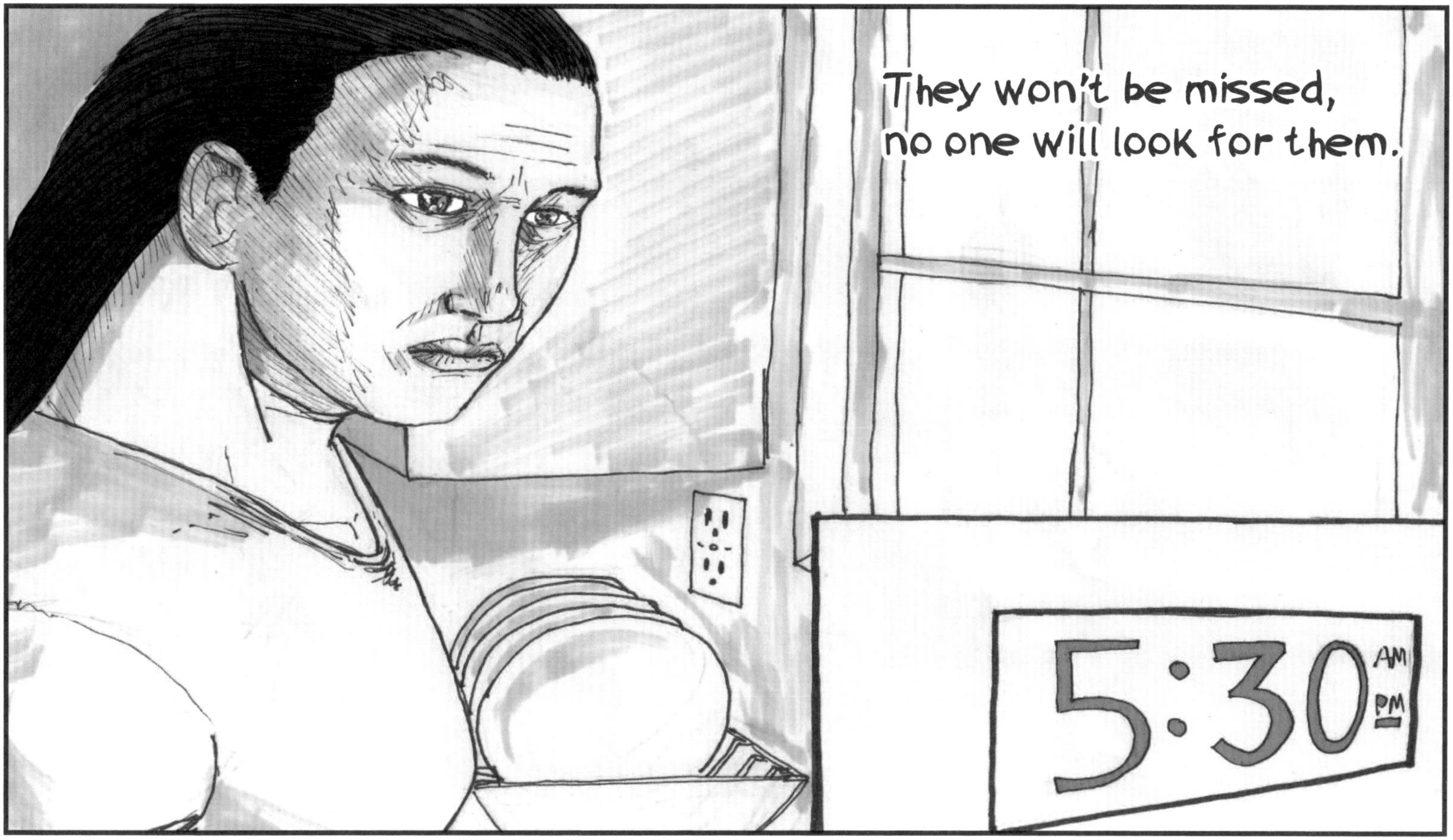
They won't be missed,
no one will look for them.
5:30 AM PM

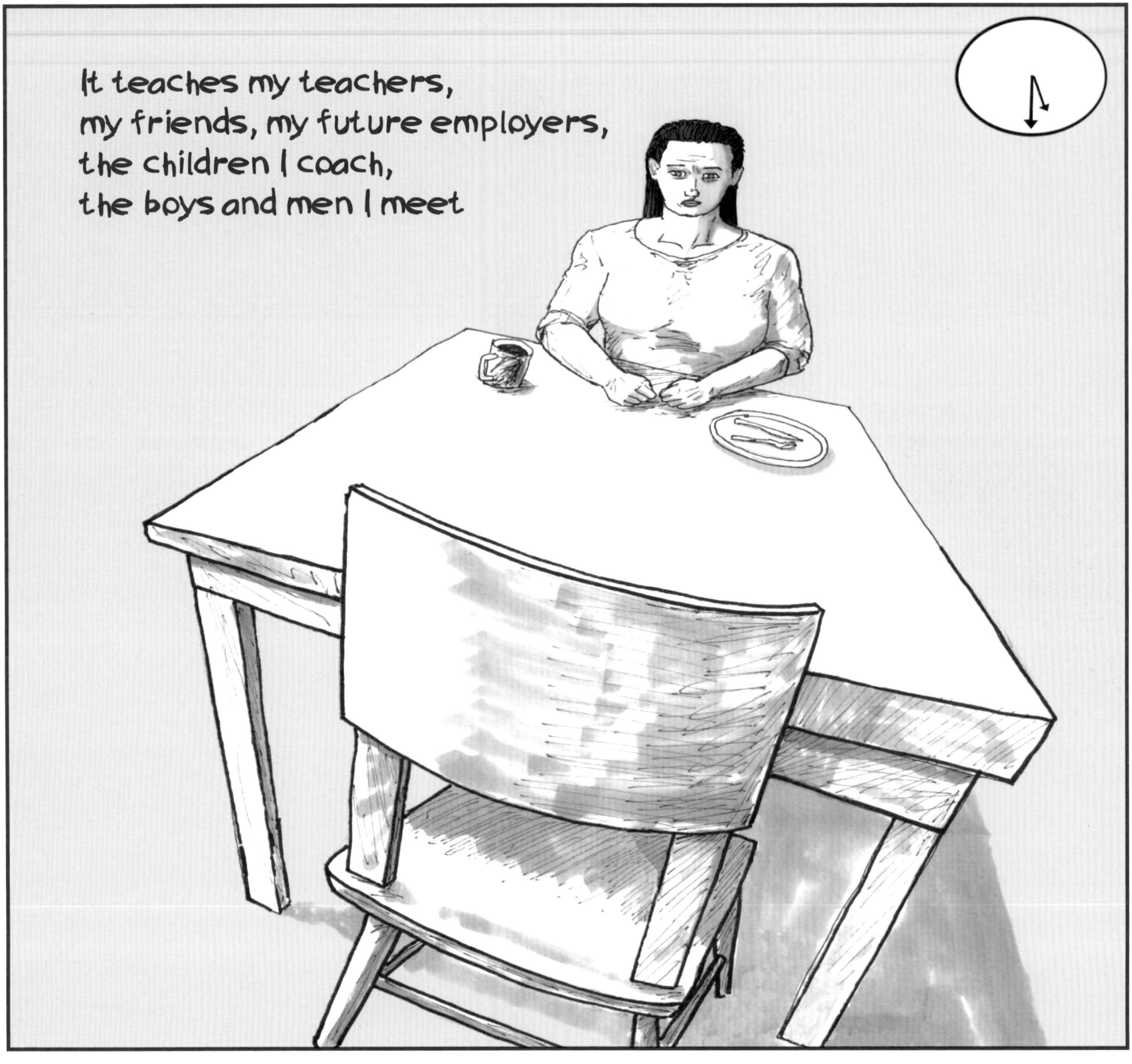
It teaches my teachers,
my friends, my future employers,
the children I coach,
the boys and men I meet

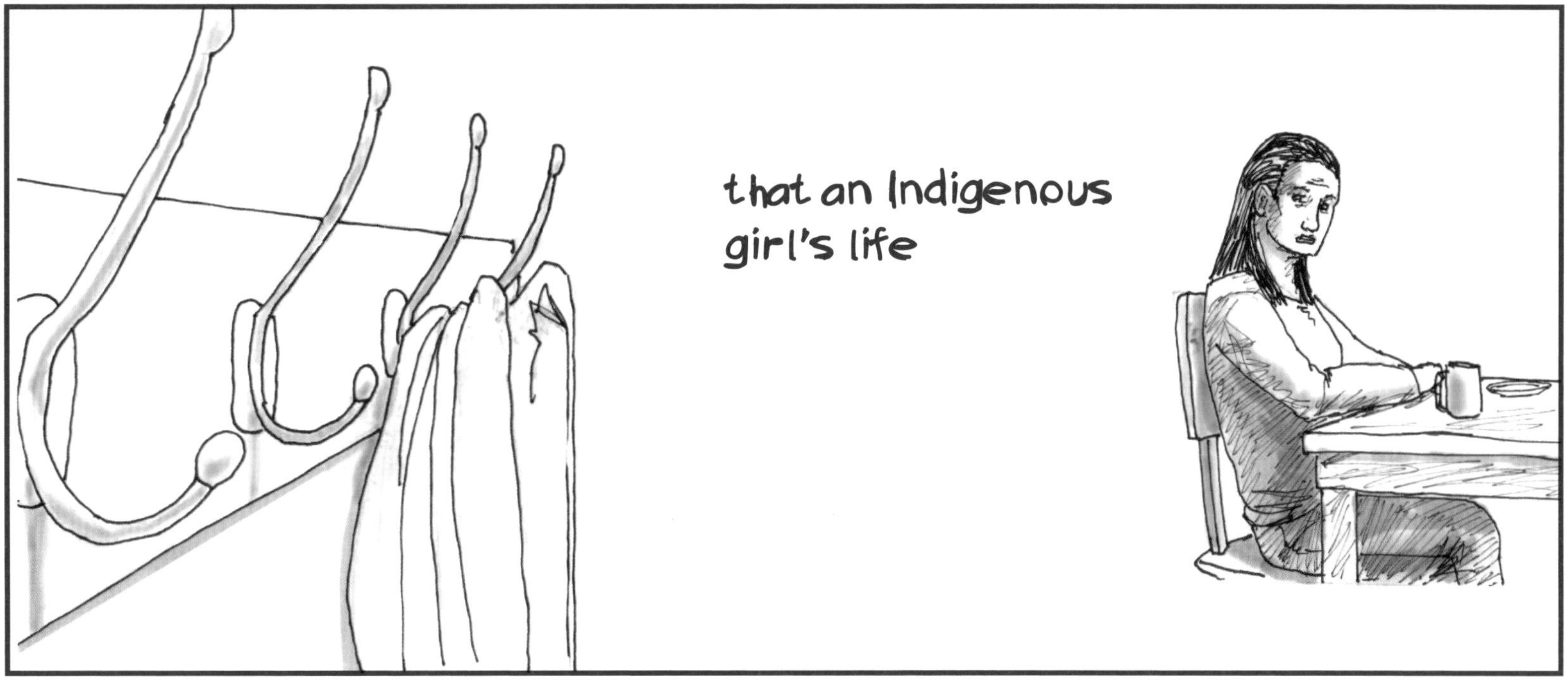
that an Indigenous girl's life

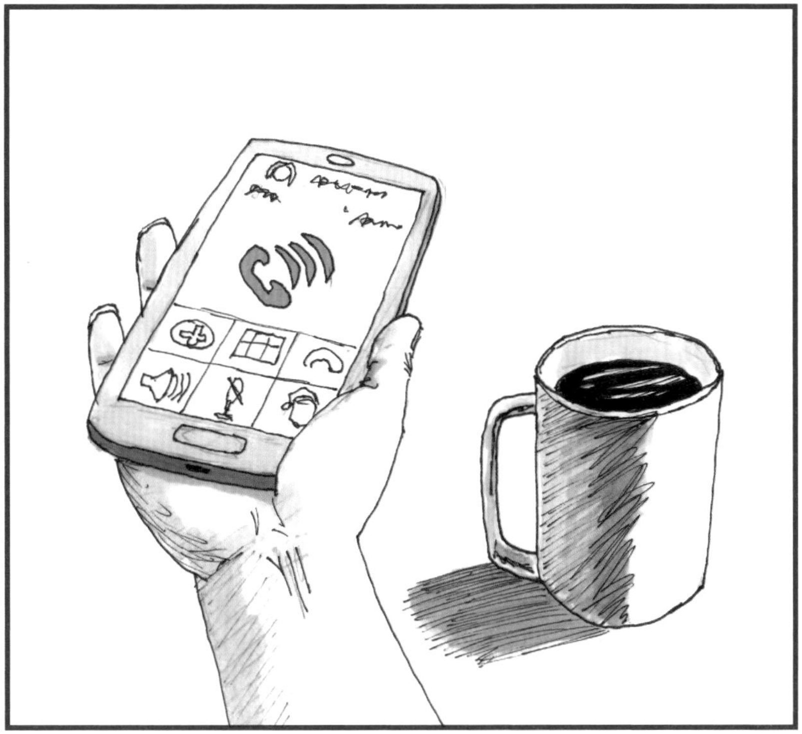

does not matter.

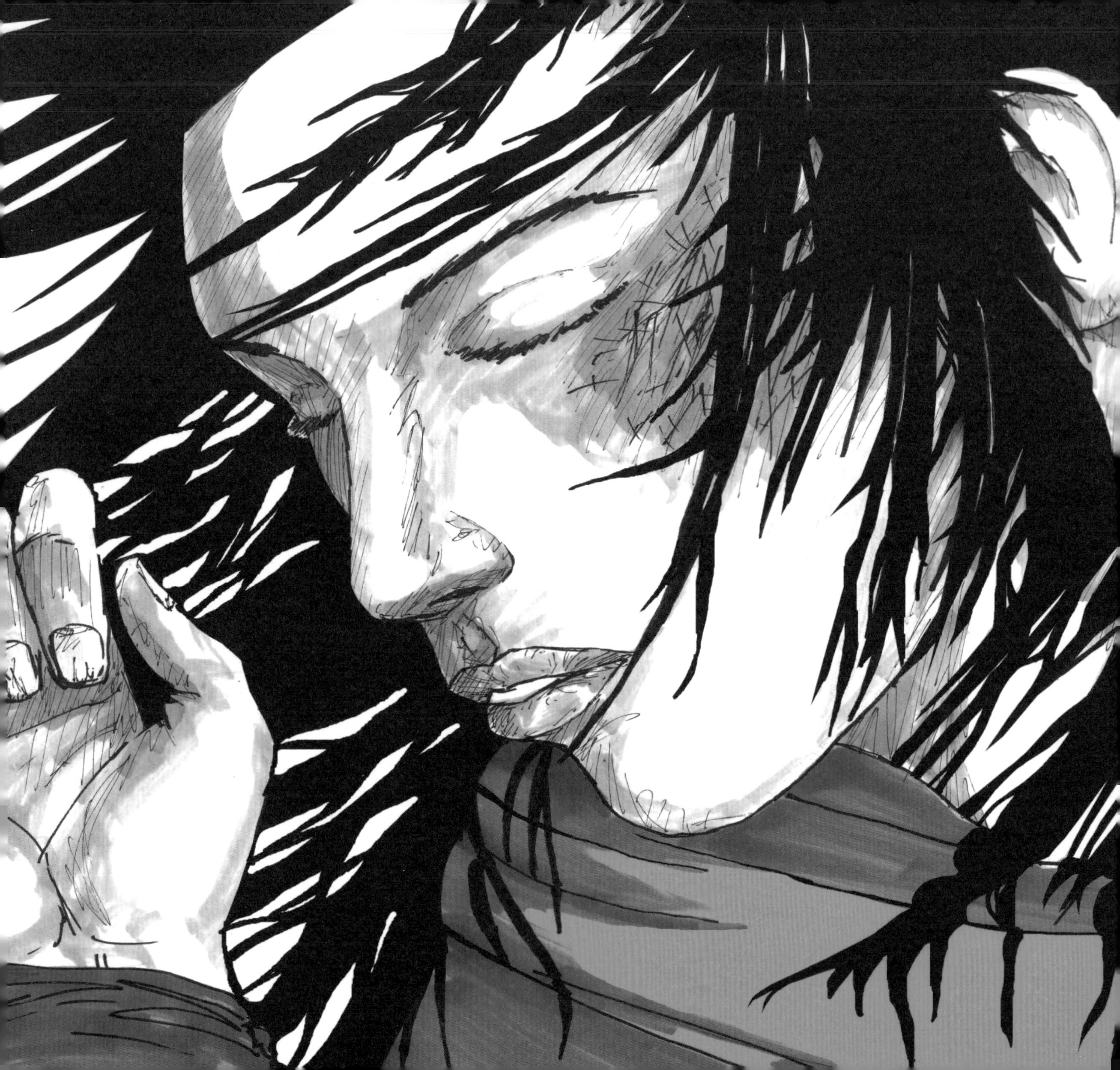

It teaches me that my life does not matter.

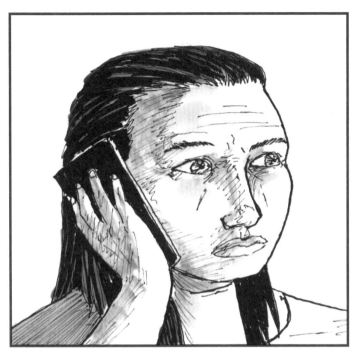

I have attached a copy of my photo.

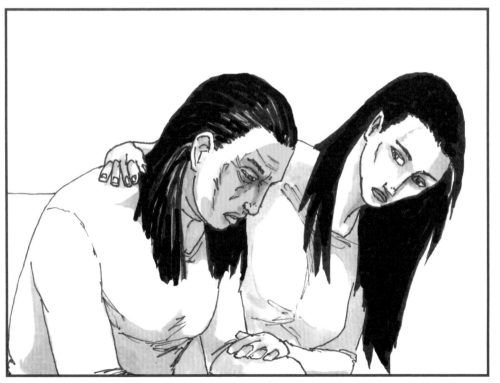

Please use this should I ever go missing.

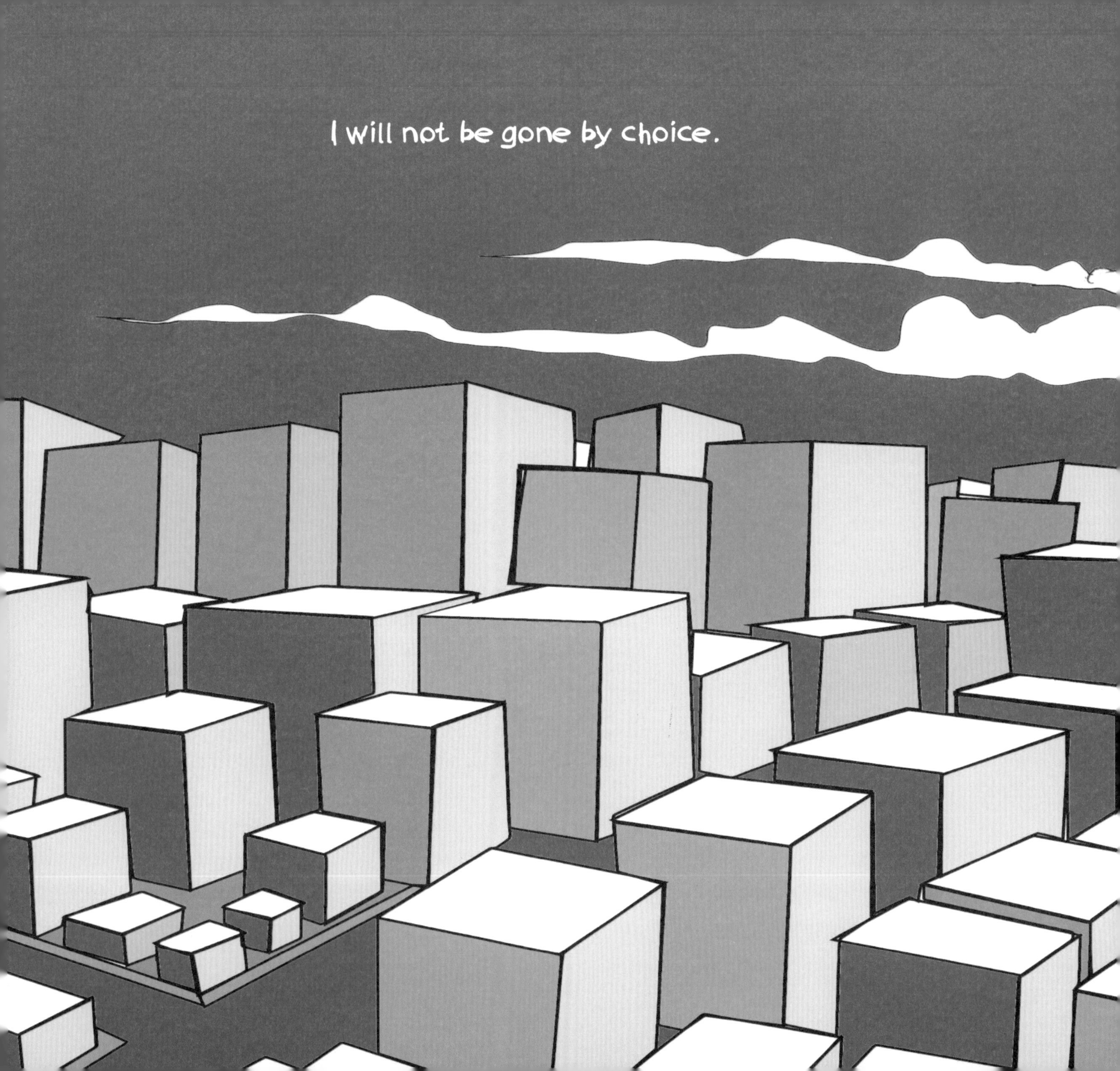
I will not be gone by choice.

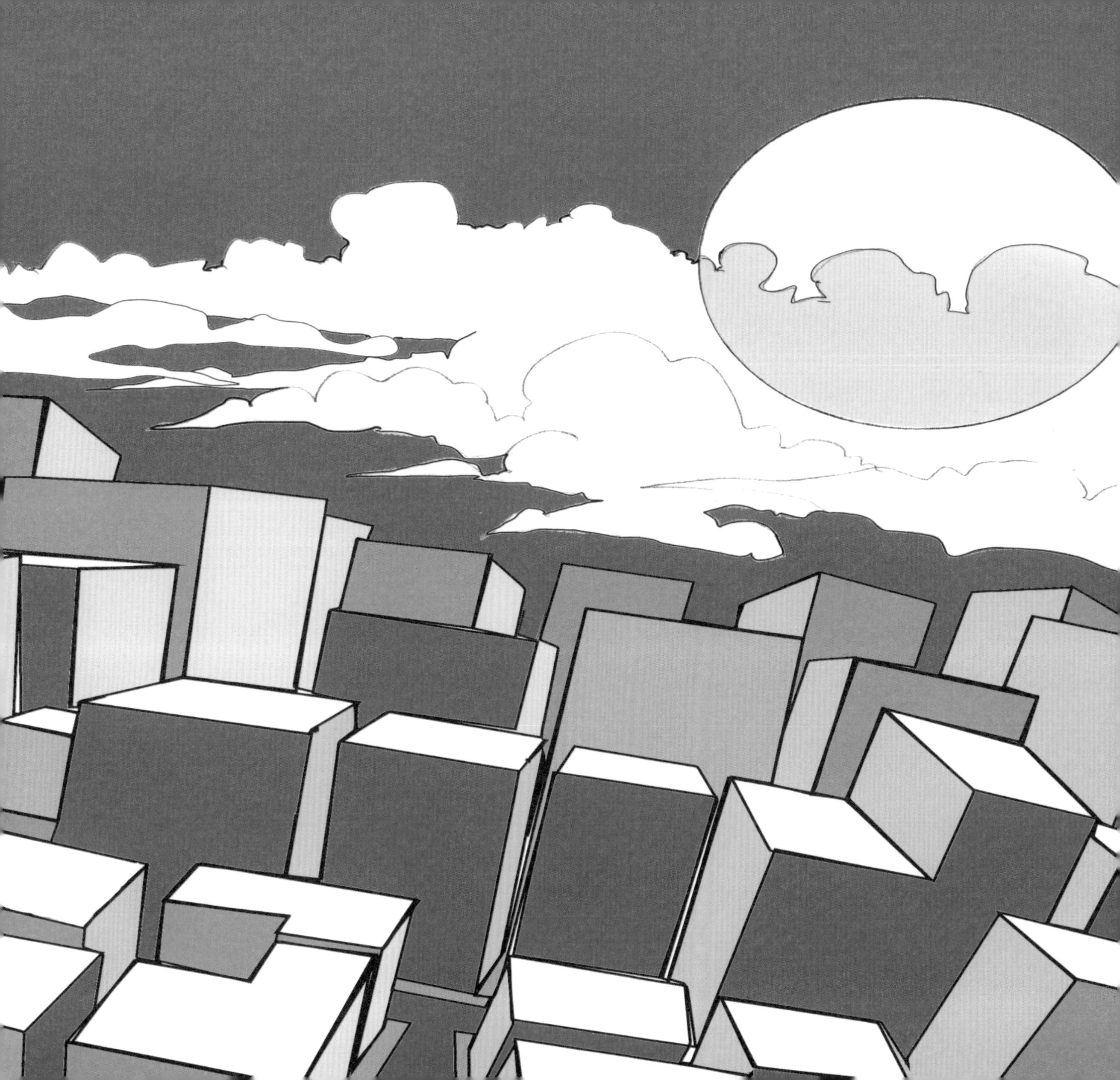

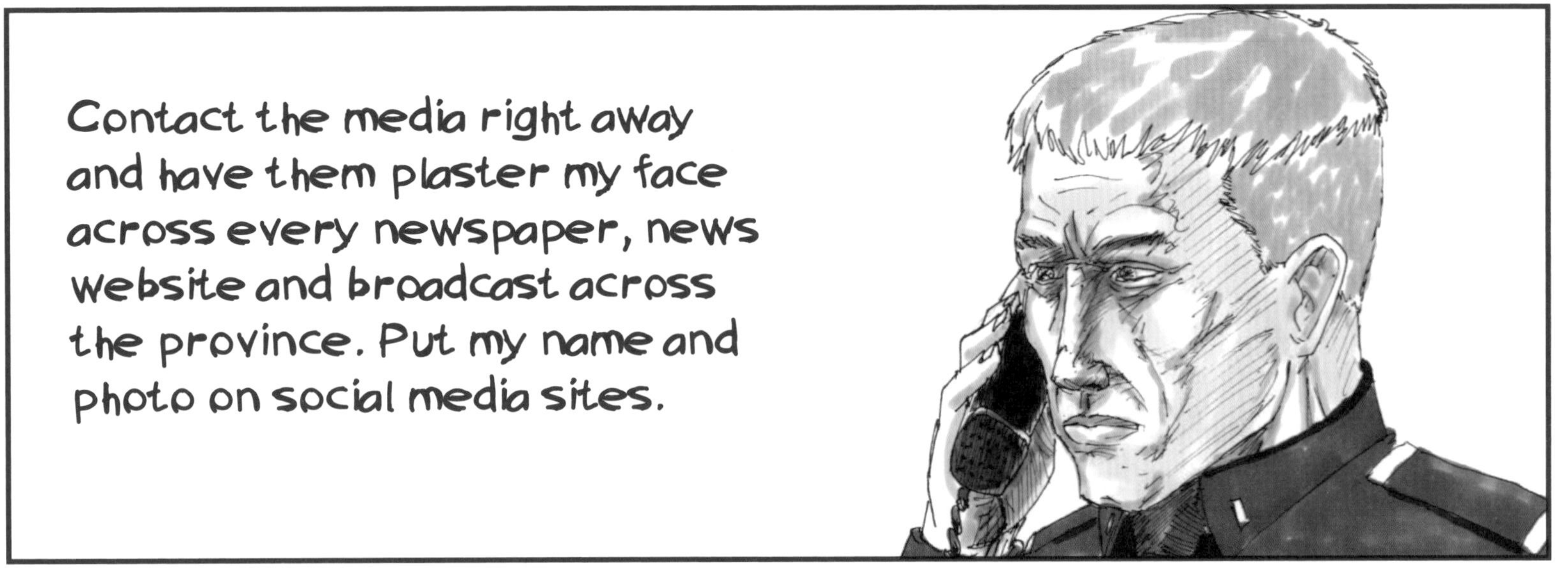
Contact the media right away and have them plaster my face across every newspaper, news website and broadcast across the province. Put my name and photo on social media sites.

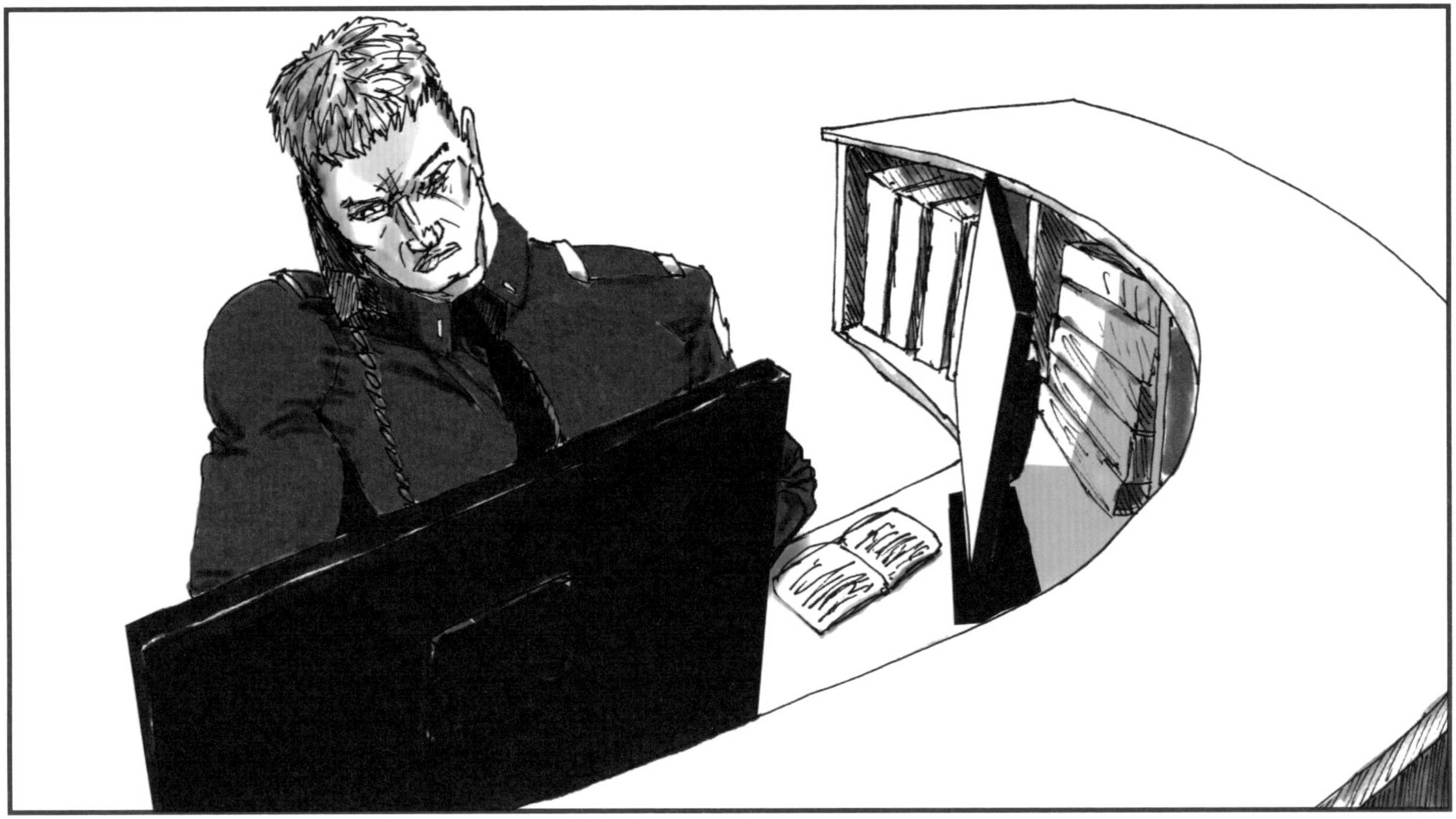

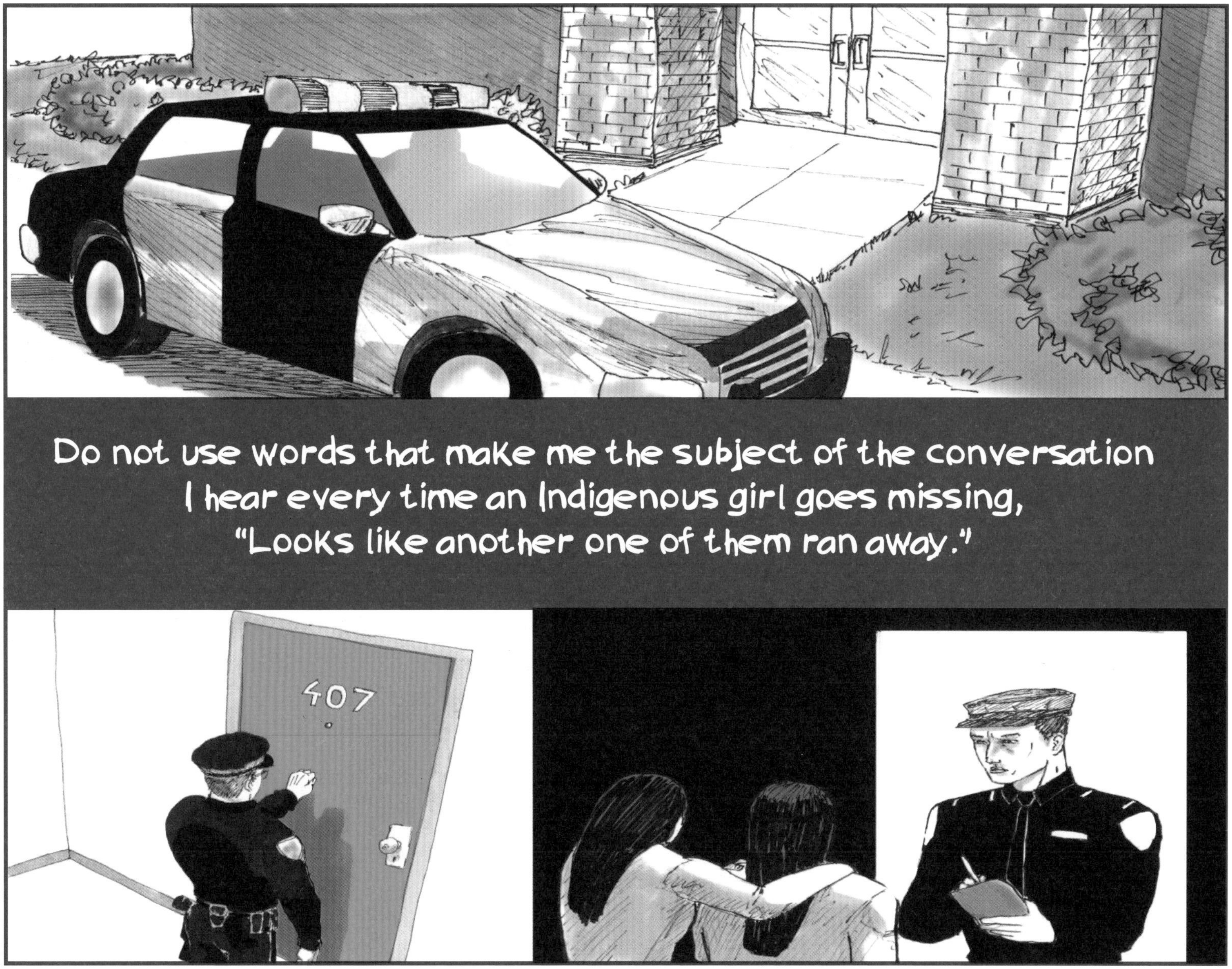
Do not use words that make me the subject of the conversation
I hear every time an Indigenous girl goes missing,
"Looks like another one of them ran away."
407

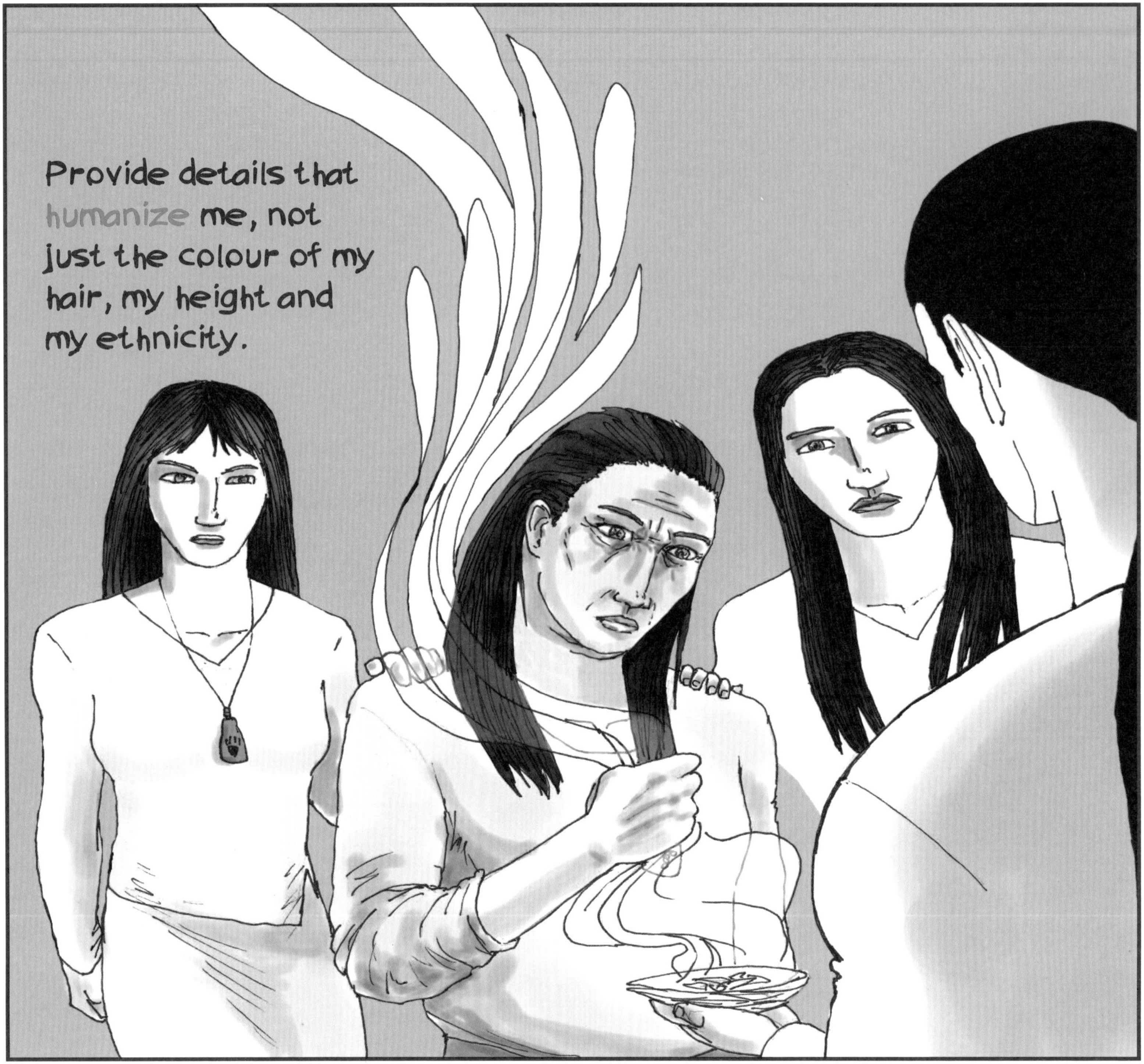
Provide details that humanize me, not just the colour of my hair, my height and my ethnicity.

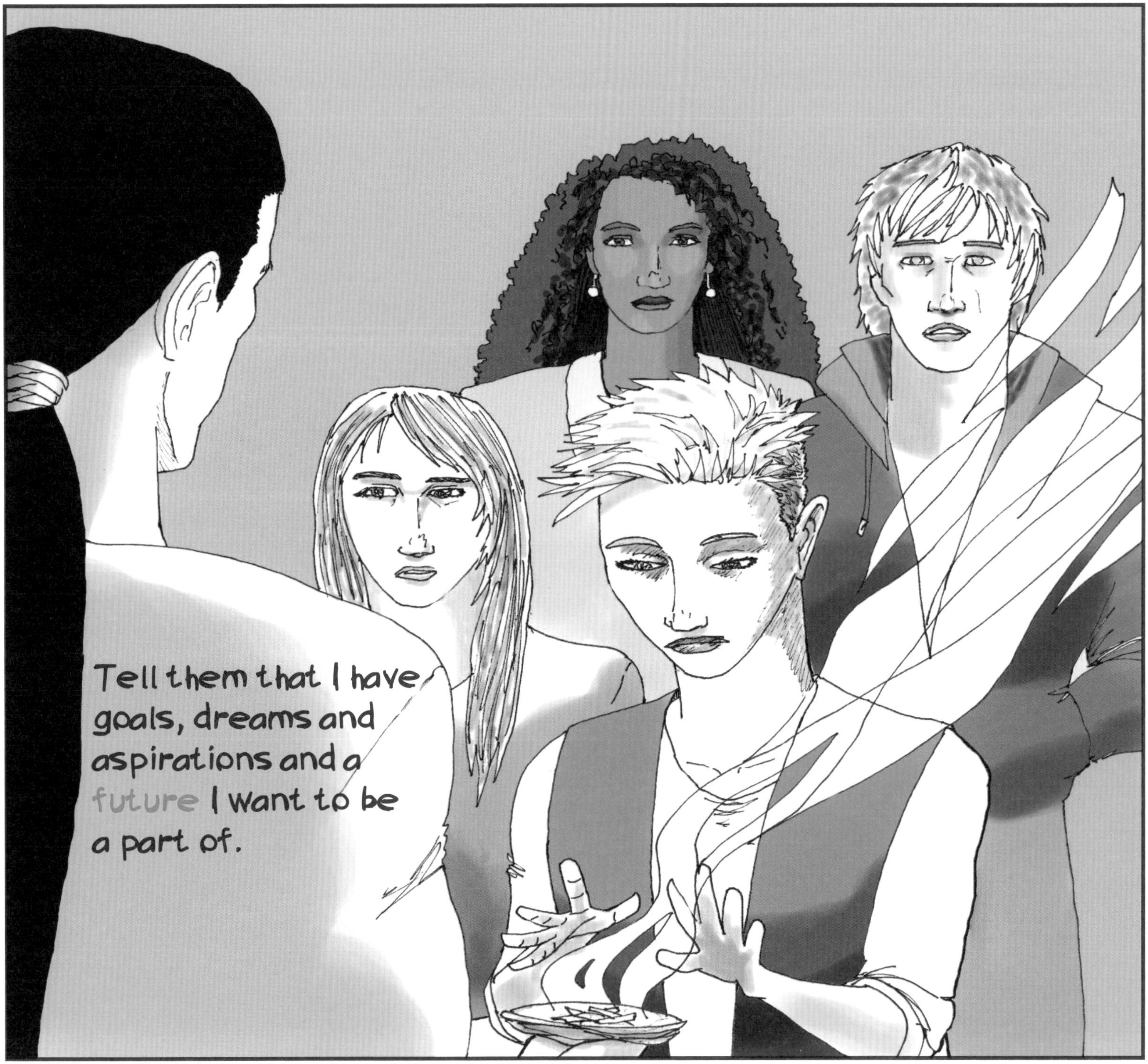
Tell them that I have goals, dreams and aspirations and a future I want to be a part of.

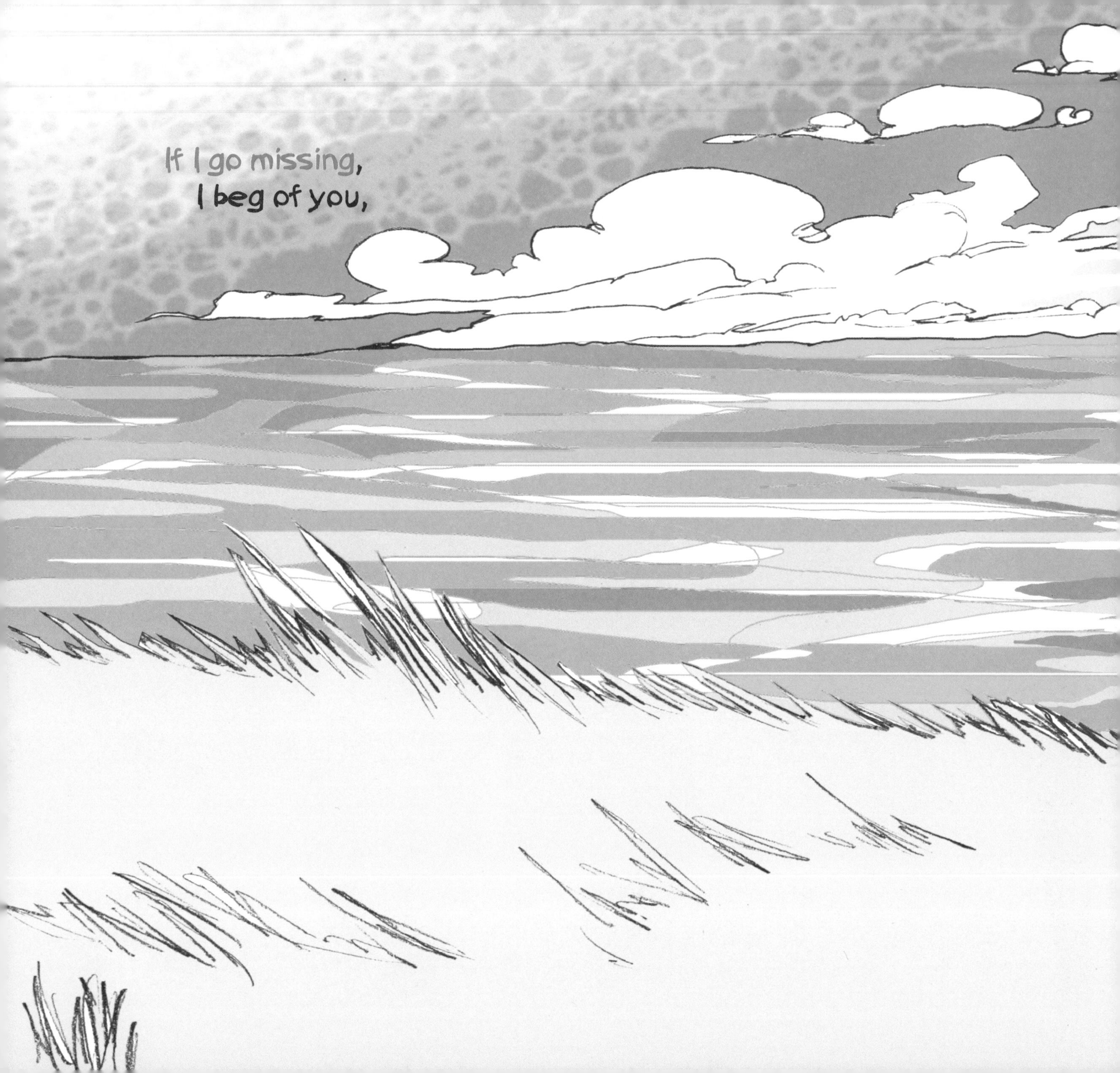
If I go missing,
I beg of you,

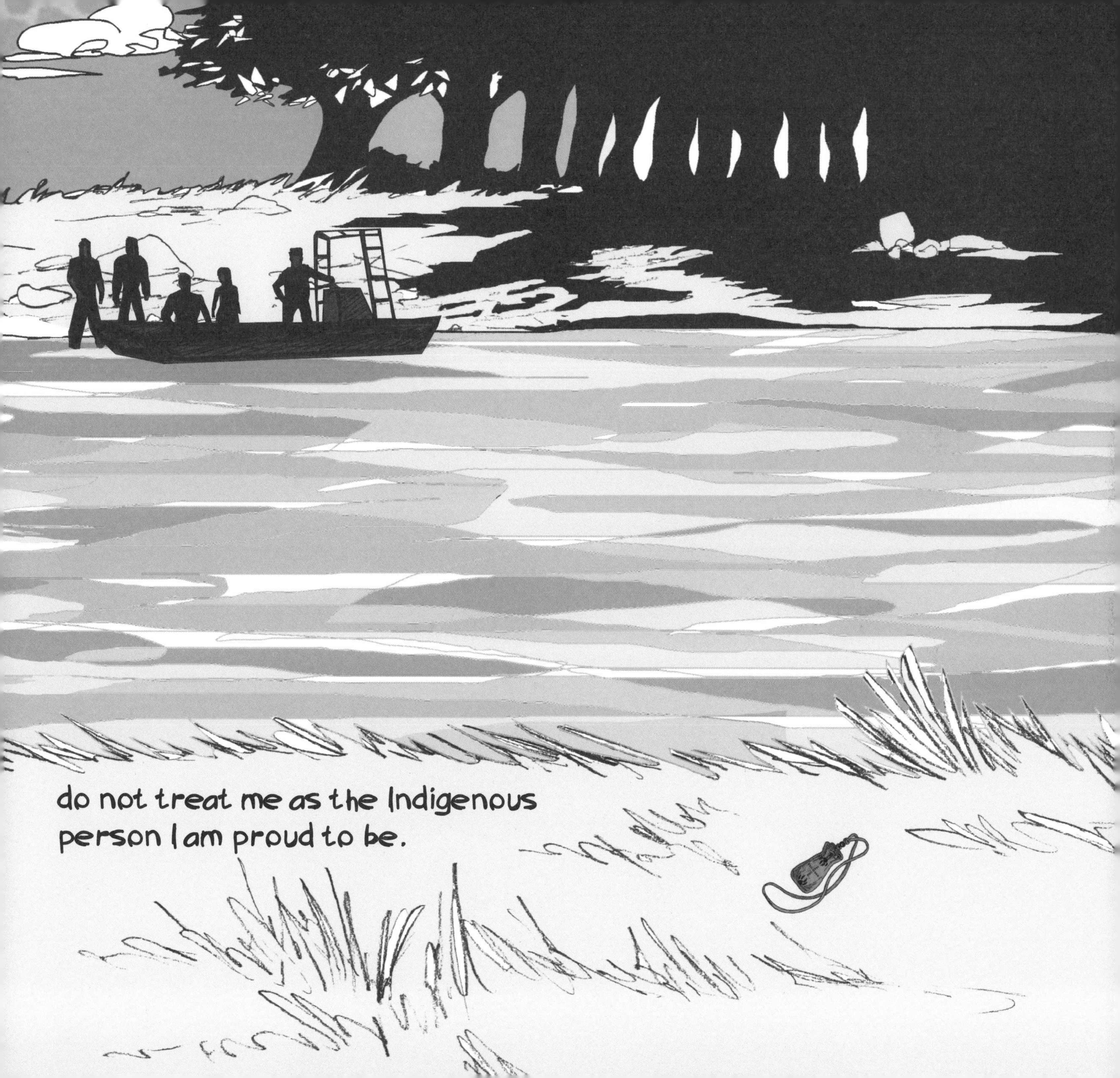

do not treat me as the Indigenous person I am proud to be.

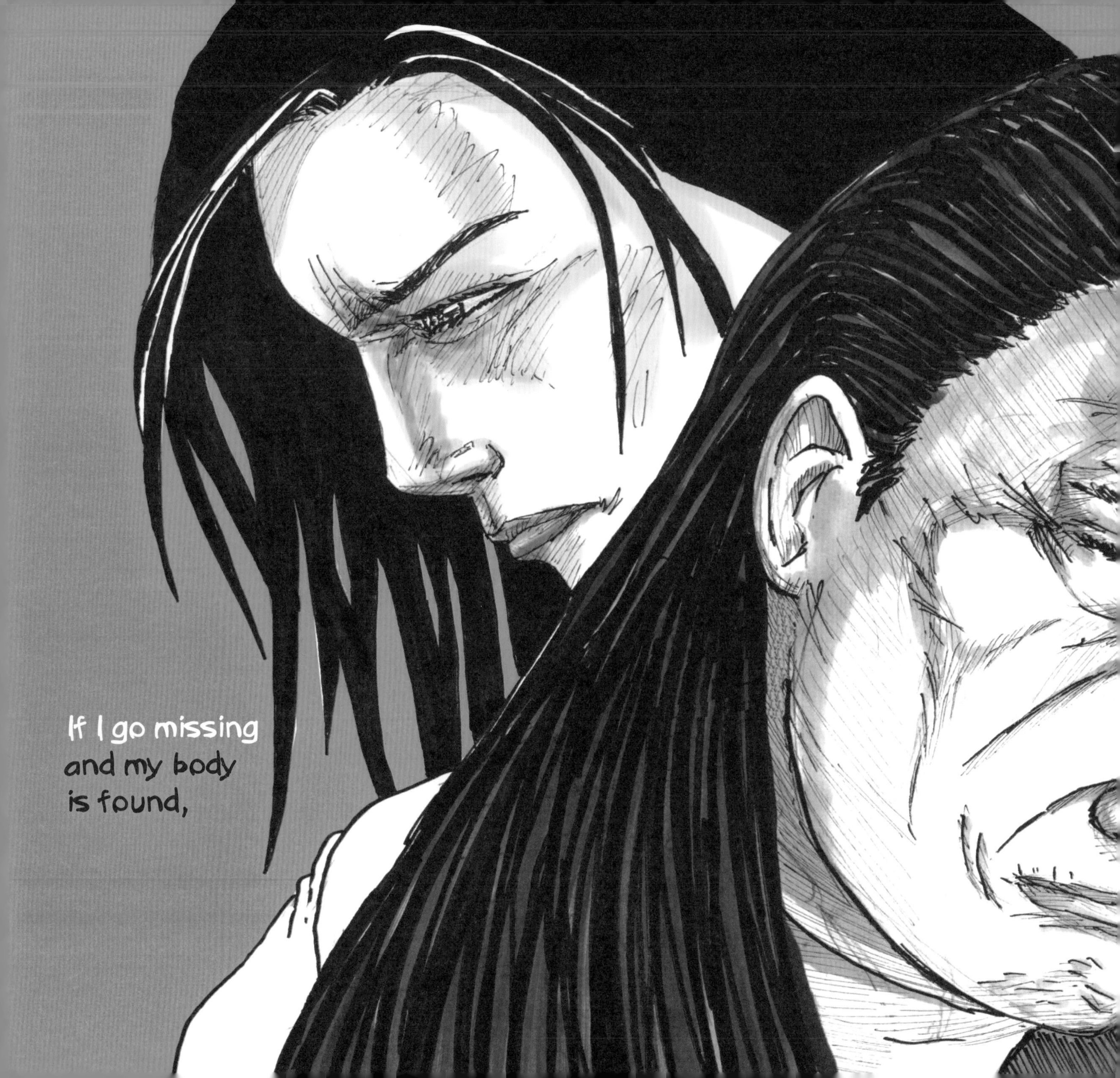
If I go missing
and my body
is found,

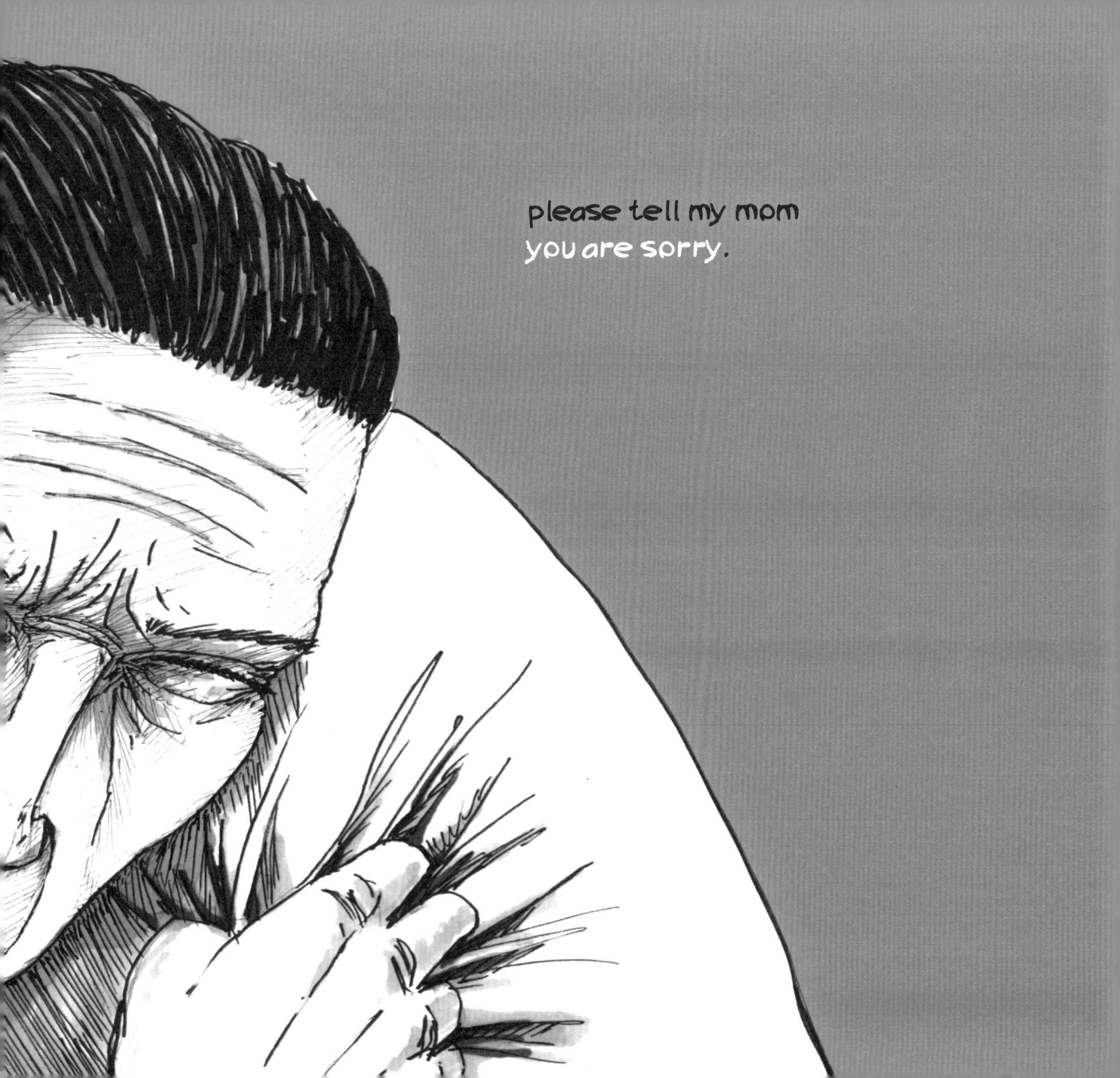

please tell my mom
you are sorry.

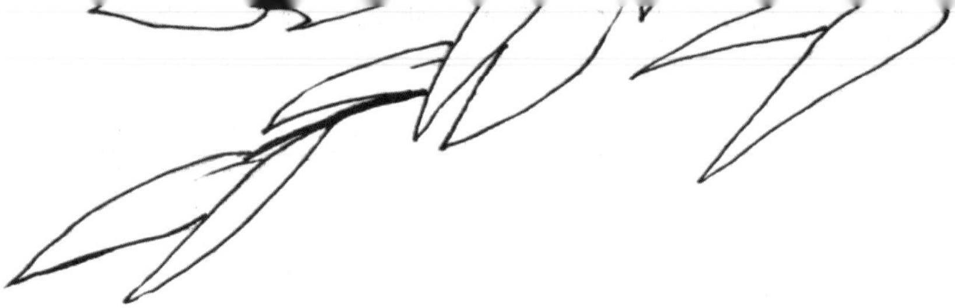

Tell her I asked to be buried in my red dress,
for I will have become just another native statistic.

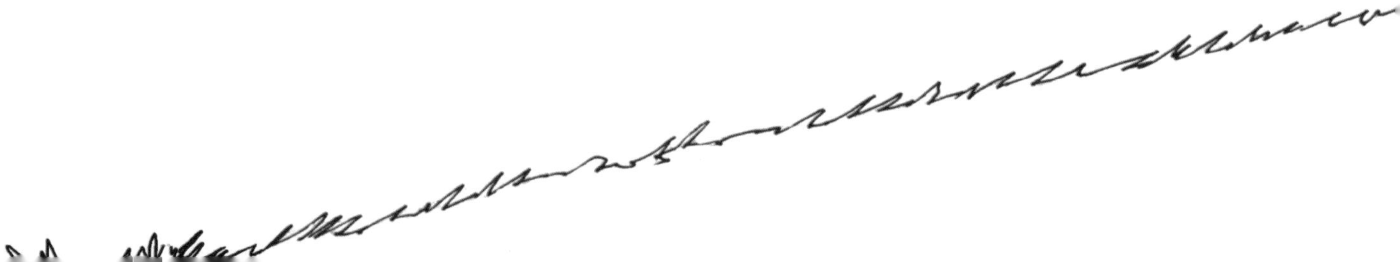

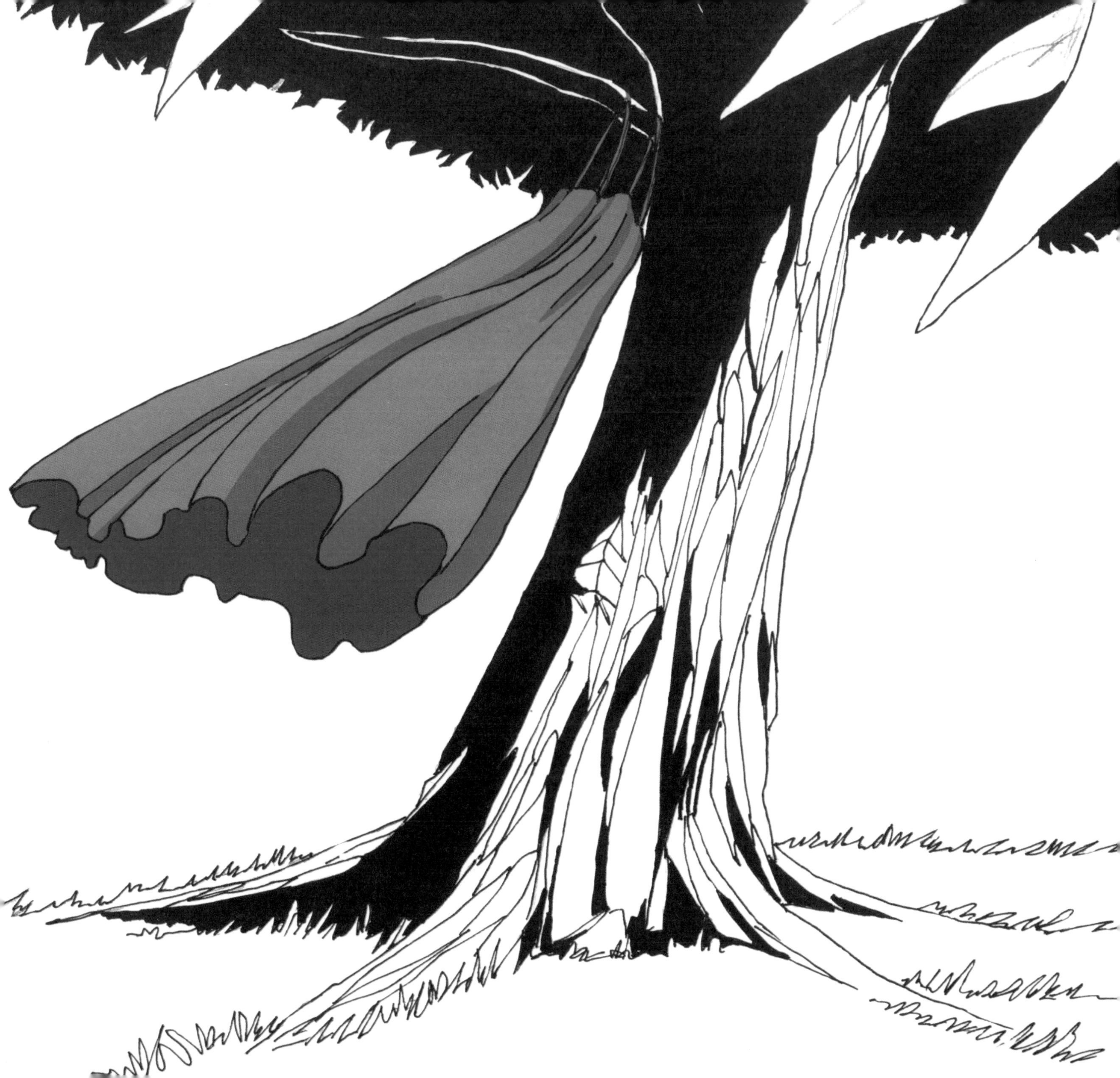

Missing and Murdered Indigenous Women and Girls is not an Indigenous issue — it's a human rights issue.

All over the world, there are groups of people who are at risk. Because of their race, background, age or orientation, their lives are seen by some as being worth less than those of others. Women make up one of these groups. They have been oppressed through history and continue to lack a voice or fair treatment in many cultures. When women go missing, searches for them are often delayed or not as wide. Crimes against them often go unsolved and unpunished. And Indigenous people across the world face assumptions and stereotypes that put their lives at risk.

Violence against Indigenous women gives us some of the most shocking facts in developed countries. In Australia, Indigenous women are victims of homicide six times more often than non-Indigenous women. They represent 16 per cent of all female murder victims, even though Indigenous people make up only 3 per cent of the Australian population. In the United States, women of colour, specifically Black women, are four times more likely to be murdered than Caucasian women.

In Canada, there have been more than 100 reports and inquiries related to violence against Indigenous women and girls, including the National Inquiry into Missing and Murdered Indigenous Women and Girls (MMIWG) launched in 2016. But no one knows for sure how many Indigenous women and girls have been murdered or gone missing. The Native Women's Association of Canada (NWAC) created a database to track these cases and its 2010 report was the first to put a number to the missing and murdered — 582. In 2013, a study identified 824 missing or murdered Indigenous women between 1946 and 2013. In the 2014 National Overview of the Royal Canadian Mounted Police, that number grew to almost 1,200 cases, just between 1980 and 2012. By the conclusion of the inquiry, the commission had gathered testimony from 1,484 family members and survivors, and 83 experts, knowledge-keepers and officials. The final report of the National Inquiry into Missing and Murdered Indigenous Women and Girls, *Reclaiming Power and Place*,* named 231 Calls for Justice directed not only at governments and institutions, but all Canadians.

Many people have studied the factors that affect MMIWG. Results suggest they might include (but are not limited to) issues of poverty, home violence and abuse, sexual violence and abuse, and addictions. These issues affect more Indigenous families than Canadian families as a whole as a direct and indirect result of Residential Schools, the Sixties Scoop and relocation projects. These government-led, racist actions removed children from their homes and placed them in boarding schools, in foster homes or with adoptive parents; they separated families, ruined lives and destroyed Indigenous cultures. The result was generations of emotional, spiritual, physical and sexual abuse, fuelled by the racist attitudes, practices and laws that stemmed from the arrival of Europeans in the Americas, when they took control of the lands and lives of Indigenous peoples. This racism has been built into systems of government and decison-making, and it continues to affect the lives of Indigenous peoples on a daily basis.

While numbers remain staggering, the conversation is beginning to shift. Rather than victim shaming and blaming women for the violence done to them, the Canadian MMIWG inquiry studies causes related to larger policies and practice.

But there is hope. It starts with awareness. Today's inquiries, art installations (such as the REDress Project by Jamie Black referred to on page 55), films, books and programs help educate the public about the issue and the devastating effect that racism has had on Indigenous families and communities.

*Source: https://www.mmiwg-ffada.ca/final-report/

Resources

For more information on the MMIWG inquiry visit the following sites:

- National Inquiry into Missing and Murdered Indigenous Women and Girls
  http://www.mmiwg-ffada.ca

- Native Women's Association of Canada — Understanding MMIWG
  https://www.nwac.ca/national-inquiry-mmiwg/understanding-mmiwg/

- Sisters in Spirit
  https://www.nwac.ca/home/policy-areas/violence-prevention-and-safety/sisters-in-spirit/

- The REDress Project
  http://www.theredressproject.org/

- Truth and Reconciliation Calls to Action
  http://trc.ca/assets/pdf/Calls_to_Action_English2.pdf

- UNDRIP — United Nations Declaration on the Rights of Indigenous Peoples
  https://www.un.org/development/desa/indigenouspeoples/declaration-on-the-rights-of-indigenous-peoples.html

About this book

IF I GO MISSING is based on a true story.

In 2016, Brianna Jonnie, then 14 years old, wrote an open letter to the Winnipeg Police Service, imploring them to "do better" when investigating cases of missing Indigenous peoples. She had noted that when a young person who looked like her went missing, it took far longer for the police service to respond — sometimes up to 16 days.

What follows is the letter that provides the text for this book (Out of respect for the missing and their families, the author has redacted [[redacted]] the names of real people included in her original letter):

March 1, 2016

Dear Chief Clunis,

My name is Brianna; I am a fourteen year old, grade nine student at Collège Jeanne-Sauvé, in South St. Vital. I would sincerely appreciate it if you could take five minutes of uninterrupted time to read what I have to say and reflect. I assure you, it is important.

Firstly, I would like to thank you and your team for finding [redacted]* and making a swift arrest. While I did not know [redacted] personally, as a high school student, I consider him a member of my community and mourn his loss. I cannot imagine the things you must see on a daily basis, nor can I fathom how difficult it must be to cope. I have the utmost respect and appreciation for the men and women who serve our city as police officers.

It was amazing to see citizens unite together in efforts to search for a missing boy. The newspapers and media were instrumental in immediately spreading news of [redacted] disappearance, bringing attention to search efforts and assisting police in asking the public for help. Deputy Chief Danny Smyth conducted himself in a most respectful manner when disclosing [redacted] had been found deceased and drugs were involved.

I have noticed missing Indigenous girls are not afforded the same courtesies — by the community, the media or the Winnipeg Police Service (WPS). [redacted] was reported missing on August 9, 2014. According to media, a WPS request for the public's help was submitted August 13th. [redacted] was reported missing on August 6, 2014 and the WPS appealed for help on August 22nd. [redacted] was reported missing on January 4, 2016 and a request for help was issued on January 15th. [redacted] however, had his image in the paper the next day; [redacted] was in online reports less than 24 hours after her disappearance and [redacted], the next day. While I acknowledge there are some differences in each of the cases, the only thing that matters in the end, is a person is missing — in many cases, a child.

I am not involved in drugs, alcohol, prostitution or other illegal activity. I am not a runaway, nor am I involved with Child and Family Services. I am an honour-roll student, a volunteer, a coach, a dancer, a friend, a daughter, a grand-daughter, a niece and a cousin. I am the only child to a young, single mom who loves me more than humanly possible and works full time trying to provide me with everything I need and want. I have goals, dreams and aspirations and a future I want to be a part of. I reside in low-income housing, my father (whom I have no contact with) is an addict and criminal and I am Indigenous. I am more likely to go missing than my peers. I am more likely than my friends to be murdered by a person unknown to me. I am more likely to be raped, assaulted or sexually violated. I cannot take public transportation or go for a walk without being approached or ogled at by men I do not know, even in the south end of the city; even during the daytime.

The Winnipeg Police Service and the media are unfortunately and likely unintentionally, making things worse. An immediate request for assistance shows the public the WPS values the life of the missing; that he/she is loved. It gives people the opportunity to mobilize search parties, creates conversations around the coffee table at work and keeps the missing person on the minds of all citizens. It increases the chance someone who knows something will come forward and the chance the individual will be found. Asking for the public's help sixteen days after an Indigenous girl goes missing is equivalent to announcing publicly her life does not matter, or at least, not as much as others. It teaches my teachers, my friends, my future employers, the children I coach, the boys and men I meet and the citizens of Winnipeg, an Indigenous girl's life does not matter. It teaches the boys and men who discard girls in rivers, beat them in back lanes and drug them at parties that Indigenous girls' lives don't matter — they won't be missed, no one will look for them. It teaches me my life does not matter.

Perhaps there are more issues at play here I am not privy to, such as rules particular to children under the care of Child and Family Services. Those children, however, have people whose heart aches for them when they go missing too. They deserve the help of the WPS, the media and the community, just as much as everyone else — maybe even more, given their lives have been filled with additional hardships and traumas. These children deserve for the WPS to exhaust all efforts to find them, as you would a non-Indigenous individual.

The colour of one's skin, their socio-economic status, or who their legal guardian is, should not determine the level of assistance and resources put in place to find them if they are missing, and yet, it does. As Chief of Police, you can do better. As an Indigenous girl, I need you to do better. I would welcome any suggestions you have in regards to ways I can help as well.

I have attached a copy of my photo. Please use this should I ever go missing — I will not be gone by choice. Ask the media for their assistance immediately and have them plaster my face across every newspaper, news website and broadcast across the province. Put my name and photo on social media sites such as Facebook and Twitter. Do not use words that make me the subject of the "looks like another one of them ran away" or "where are their parents?" conversation that I hear every time an Indigenous girl goes missing. Provide details that humanize me, not just the colour of my hair, my height and my ethnicity. Provide my mom with the resources she needs to mobilize search teams and seek support. She will be fierce, strong and determined to find me, but terrified, numb and broken on the inside. If I go missing and the WPS has not changed the behaviours I have brought to your attention, I beg of you, do not treat me as the Indigenous person I am proud to be. My mom needs me, and I want to have my future.

And if I do go missing and my body is found, please tell my mom you are sorry. Tell her I asked to be buried in my red dress, for I will have become just another native statistic.

Sincerely and respectfully,

Brianna Jonnie

CC: The Honourable Greg Selinger, Premier
                Honourable Kerri Irvin-Ross, Minister of Family Services
                Honourable Gord Mackintosh, Minister of Justice and Attorney General
                Honourable Eric Robinson, Minister of Aboriginal and Northern Affairs
                Mayor Brian Bowman, City of Winnipeg
                Mr. Bob Cox, Publisher of the Winnipeg Free Press
                Mr. Paul Samyn, Editor of the Winnipeg Free Press

Encl.

About Brianna Jonnie

BRIANNA JONNIE, Ojibwe, is a member of Roseau River First Nation, Manitoba. As a young girl, Brianna Jonnie discovered the REDress art installation in Winnipeg. Red dresses were hung from trees on a university campus, representing the thousands of Missing and Murdered Indigenous Women and Girls in Canada. It was an issue that caught her attention. After her letter to the Winnipeg Police went viral, Brianna wanted to do more. She joined a youth empowerment group — Strong Girls, Strong World — to speak to young people about healthy relationships and setting healthy boundaries.

Two years later, Brianna questioned Prime Minister Justin Trudeau at a town hall at the University of Winnipeg about the MMIWG Inquiry: "When so many no longer trust the process, how will you measure — in quantifiable terms — whether the inquiry into murdered and missing Indigenous women and girls is successful?" As a result of her question, Brianna received more media attention. A local producer initiated a film about Brianna, and Brianna had the chance to meet the artist of the REDress Project that started it all. Brianna has been awarded the City of Winnipeg's Youth Role Model Award in the advocacy category, and she continues to walk a path of courage. She is a dancer, coach, friend, daughter and student. Brianna lives in Winnipeg.

About Nahanni Shingoose

NAHANNI SHINGOOSE, Ojibwe and Irish, is a member of Roseau River First Nation, Manitoba. Nahanni is Brianna's auntie. She is also an award-winning educator, author and artist. Nahanni's career is dedicated to working with and for Indigenous youth. She also works for the National Film Board of Canada as a lead writer and emerging film maker. She hopes to become a role model for her own two daughters, Sage and Ziibii, and to her students. Nahanni's paternal grandmother and all six of her siblings are residential school survivors. She is the author of the YA novel *Powwow Summer*. Nahanni lives in Stoney Creek, Ontario.

About Neal Shannacappo

NEAL SHANNACAPPO is a Nakawe (Saulteaux) graphic novelist from Ditibineya-Ziibiing (Rolling River First Nation) in Manitoba. He is Migizi odoodeman (Eagle Clan) He has published stories in the Indigenous anthologies *Sovereign Traces Volume 1: Not (Just) (An)other* and *Sovereign Traces Volume 2: Relational Constellation.* Neal is also the creator of the graphic novel *The Krillian Key.* His book *Mashkawide'e (Has a strong heart)* was published by Senator Kim Pate. Throughout his work, Neal celebrates the vibrant artistic community and culture of Indigenous people, paying homage to past and present and to the spiritual. He lives in Ottawa, Ontario.